PRAXIS

ENGLISH LANGUAGE ARTS: CONTENT KNOWLEDGE 5038

By: Sharon A. Wynne, M.S.

XAMonline, INC.
Boston

To obtain permission(s) to use the material from this work for any purpose including workshops or seminars, please submit a written request to:

XAMonline, Inc.
21 Orient Avenue
Melrose, MA 02176
Toll Free 1-800-301-4647
Email: info@xamonline.com
Web: www.xamonline.com
Fax: 1-617-583-5552

Library of Congress Cataloging-in-Publication Data

Wynne, Sharon A.
　　PRAXIS English Language Arts: Content Knowledge 5038 / Sharon A. Wynne
　　ISBN 978-1-60787-627-4
　　1. English Language Arts: Content Knoweldge 5038
　　2. Study Guides
　　3. PRAXIS
　　4. Teachers' Certification & Licensure
　　5. Careers

Disclaimer:

The opinions expressed in this publication are the sole works of XAMonline and were created independently from the National Education Association, Educational Testing Service, or any State Department of Education, National Evaluation Systems or other testing affiliates.

Between the time of publication and printing, state specific standards as well as testing formats and Web site information may change and therefore would not be included in part or in whole within this product. Sample test questions are developed by XAMonline and reflect content similar to that on real tests; however, they are not former test questions. XAMonline assembles content that aligns with state standards but makes no claims nor guarantees teacher candidates a passing score. Numerical scores are determined by testing companies such as NES or ETS and then are compared with individual state standards. A passing score varies from state to state.

Printed in the United States of America　　　　　　　　　　　　　　　　œ-1

PRAXIS English Language Arts: Content Knowledge 5038
ISBN: 978-1-60787-627-4

Table of Contents

SECTION I

SECTION II
LANGUAGE USE AND VOCABULARY 65

SECTION III
WRITING, SPEAKING, AND LISTENING 83

SAMPLE TEST

PRAXIS
ENGLISH LANGUAGE ARTS: CONTENT KNOWLEDGE 5038

MEET THE AUTHORS

Heather M. Hilliard

Earning her bachelor's degree in New Orleans and her two masters degrees from the University of Pittsburgh, Heather M. Hilliard serves as an Adjunct Professor for her undergraduate alma mater, Tulane University. From teaching – both at the collegiate level as well as special courses at a leading independent high school – to her corporate endeavors, she has consciously focused aspects of her career and volunteerism on education. She has received several commendations for her achievements, has been inducted into the national honor society for public health and is one of fewer than 1,000 internationally Certified Emergency Managers in the world. She has published on a variety of topics and edited textbooks as well as other fiction and non-fiction work and focuses on strategic communications and improvements for clients – including writing and editing for XAMonline preparation content and tests including Advanced Placement exams, CLEP materials, and the SAT.

Jessica Egan

With a Master's Degree in English Education from Florida State University, Jessica Egan has expertise in the areas of literature, linguistics, and educational psychology. Jessica has worked as an instructional technologist and has experience in teaching secondary English, English as a Second Language (ESL), college-level composition and Adult Basic Education (ABE). She has authored lesson plans, teacher certification materials, and test preparation texts.

John Keefe

John Keefe is an author and editor from Chicago, Illinois. A graduate of Columbia College Chicago, John Keefe has written fiction and non-fiction for publications such as Chicago Literati, Hair Trigger Magazine, and websites like Cracked.com. He is also an actor and playwright.

ABOUT XAMONLINE

XAMonline—A Specialty Teacher Certification Company

Created in 1996, XAMonline was the first company to publish study guides for state-specific teacher certification examinations. Founder Sharon Wynne found it frustrating that materials were not available for teacher certification preparation and decided to create the first single, state-specific guide. XAMonline has grown into a company of over 1,800 contributors and writers and offers over 300 titles for the entire PRAXIS series and every state examination. No matter what state you plan on teaching in, XAMonline has a unique teacher certification study guide just for you.

XAMonline—Value and Innovation

We are committed to providing value and innovation. Our print-on-demand technology allows us to be the first in the market to reflect changes in test standards and user feedback as they occur. Our guides are written by experienced teachers who are experts in their fields. And our content reflects the highest standards of quality. Comprehensive practice tests with varied levels of rigor means that your study experience will closely match the actual in-test experience.

To date, XAMonline has helped nearly 600,000 teachers pass their certification or licensing exams. Our commitment to preparation exceeds simply providing the proper material for study—it extends to helping teachers **gain mastery** of the subject matter, giving them the **tools** to become the most effective classroom leaders possible, and ushering today's students toward a **successful future**.

ABOUT THIS STUDY GUIDE

Purpose of This Guide

Is there a little voice inside of you saying, "Am I ready?" Our goal is to replace that little voice and remove all doubt with a new voice that says, "I AM READY. **Bring it on!**" by offering the highest quality of teacher certification study guides.

Organization of Content

You will see that while every test may start with overlapping general topics, each is very unique in the skills they wish to test. Only XAMonline presents custom content that analyzes deeper than a title, a subarea, or an objective. Only XAMonline presents content and sample test assessments along with **focus statements**, the deepest-level rationale and interpretation of the skills that are unique to the exam.

Title and field number of test
→Each exam has its own name and number. XAMonline's guides are written to give you the content you need to know for the specific exam you are taking. You can be confident when you buy our guide that it contains the information you need to study for the specific test you are taking.

Subareas
→These are the major content categories found on the exam. XAMonline's guides are written to cover all of the subareas found in the test frameworks developed for the exam.

Objectives
→These are standards that are unique to the exam and represent the main subcategories of the subareas/content categories. XAMonline's guides are written to address every specific objective required to pass the exam.

Focus statements
→These are examples and interpretations of the objectives. You find them in parenthesis directly following the objective. They provide detailed examples of the range, type, and level of content that appear on the test questions. **Only XAMonline's guides drill down to this level.**

How Do We Compare with Our Competitors?
XAMonline—drills down to the focus statement level.
CliffsNotes and REA—organized at the objective level
Kaplan—provides only links to content
MoMedia—content not specific to the state test

Each subarea is divided into manageable sections that cover the specific skill areas. Explanations are easy to understand and thorough. You'll find that every test answer contains a rejoinder so if you need a refresher or further review after taking the test, you'll know exactly to which section you must return.

How to Use This Book
Our informal polls show that most people begin studying up to eight weeks prior to the test date, so start early. Then ask yourself some questions: How much do you really know? Are you coming to the test straight from your teacher-education program or are you having to review subjects you haven't considered in ten years? Either way, take a **diagnostic or assessment test** first. Also, spend time on sample tests so that you become accustomed to the way the actual test will appear.

This guide comes with an online diagnostic test of 30 questions found online at *www.XAMonline.com*. It is a little boot camp to get you up for the task and reveal things about your compendium of knowledge in general. Although this guide is structured to follow the order of the test, you are not required to study in that order. By finding a time-management and study plan that fits your life you will be more effective. The results of your diagnostic or self-assessment test can be a guide for how to manage your time and point you toward an area that needs more attention.

After taking the diagnostic exam, fill out the **Personalized Study Plan** page at the beginning of each chapter. Review the competencies and skills covered in that chapter and check the boxes that apply to your study needs. If there are sections you already know you can skip, check the "skip it" box. Taking this step will give you a study plan for each chapter.

Week	Activity
8 weeks prior to test	Take a diagnostic test found at www.XAMonline.com
6-3 weeks prior to test	For each of these four weeks, choose a content area to study. You don't have to go in the order of the book. It may be that you start with the content that needs the most review. Alternately, you may want to ease yourself into plan by starting with the most familiar material.
2 weeks prior to test	Take the sample test, score it, and create a review plan for the final week before the test.
1 week prior to test	Following your plan (which will likely be aligned with the areas that need the most review) go back and study the sections that align with the questions you may have gotten wrong. Then go back and study the sections related to the questions you answered correctly. If need be, create flashcards and drill yourself on any area that makes you anxious.

HELPFUL HINTS

Study Tips

1. **You are what you eat.** Certain foods aid the learning process by releasing natural memory enhancers called CCKs (cholecystokinin) composed of tryptophan, choline, and phenylalanine. All of these chemicals enhance the neurotransmitters associated with memory and certain foods release memory enhancing chemicals. A light meal or snacks of one of the following foods fall into this category:

   - Milk
   - Rice
   - Eggs
   - Fish
   - Nuts and seeds
   - Oats
   - Turkey

   The better the connections, the more you comprehend!

2. **See the forest for the trees.** In other words, get the concept before you look at the details. One way to do this is to take notes as you read, paraphrasing or summarizing in your own words. Putting the concept in terms that are comfortable and familiar may increase retention.

3. **Question authority.** Ask why, why, why? Pull apart written material paragraph by paragraph and don't forget the captions under the illustrations. For example, if a heading reads *Stream Erosion* put it in the form of a question (Why do streams erode? What is stream erosion?) then find the answer within the material. If you train your mind to think in this manner you will learn more and prepare yourself for answering test questions.

4. **Play mind games.** Using your brain for reading or puzzles keeps it flexible. Even with a limited amount of time your brain can take in data (much like a computer) and store it for later use. In ten minutes you can: read two paragraphs (at least), quiz yourself with flash cards, or review notes. Even if you don't fully understand something on the first pass, your mind stores it for recall, which is why frequent reading or review increases chances of retention and comprehension.

5. **Place yourself in exile and set the mood.** Set aside a particular place and time to study that best suits your personal needs and biorhythms. If you're a night person, burn the midnight oil. If you're a morning person set yourself up with some coffee and get to it. Make your study time and place as free from distraction as possible and surround yourself with what you need, be it silence or music. Studies have shown that music can aid in concentration, absorption, and retrieval of information. Not all music, though. Classical music is said to work best

6. **Get pointed in the right direction.** Use arrows to point to important passages or pieces of information. It's easier to read than a page full of yellow highlights. Highlighting can be used sparingly, but add an arrow to the margin to call attention to it.

7. **Check your budget.** You should at least review all the content material before your test, but allocate the most amount of time to the areas that need the most refreshing. It sounds obvious, but it's easy to forget. You can use the study rubric above to balance your study budget.

8. **The pen is mightier than the sword.** Learn to take great notes. A by-product of our modern culture is that we have grown accustomed to getting our information in short doses. We've subconsciously trained ourselves to assimilate information into neat little packages. Messy notes fragment the flow of information. Your notes can be much clearer with proper formatting. *The Cornell Method* is one such format. This method was popularized in *How to Study in College*, Ninth Edition, by Walter Pauk. You can benefit from the method without purchasing an additional book by simply looking up the method online. Below is a sample of how *The Cornell Method* can be adapted for use with this guide.

The proctor will write the start time where it can be seen and then, later, provide the time remaining, typically fifteen minutes before the end of the test.

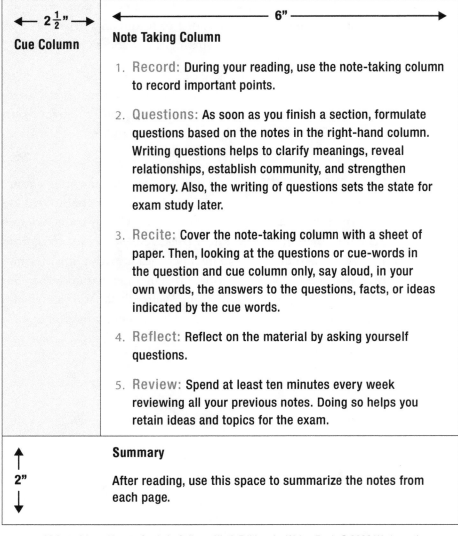

← 2½" → Cue Column	← 6" → Note Taking Column
	1. Record: During your reading, use the note-taking column to record important points.
	2. Questions: As soon as you finish a section, formulate questions based on the notes in the right-hand column. Writing questions helps to clarify meanings, reveal relationships, establish community, and strengthen memory. Also, the writing of questions sets the state for exam study later.
	3. Recite: Cover the note-taking column with a sheet of paper. Then, looking at the questions or cue-words in the question and cue column only, say aloud, in your own words, the answers to the questions, facts, or ideas indicated by the cue words.
	4. Reflect: Reflect on the material by asking yourself questions.
	5. Review: Spend at least ten minutes every week reviewing all your previous notes. Doing so helps you retain ideas and topics for the exam.
↑ 2" ↓	Summary After reading, use this space to summarize the notes from each page.

*Adapted from How to Study in College, Ninth Edition, by Walter Pauk, ©2008 Wadsworth

Testing Tips

1. **Get smart, play dumb.** Sometimes a question is just a question. No one is out to trick you, so don't assume that the test writer is looking for something other than what was asked. Stick to the question as written and don't overanalyze.

2. **Do a double take.** Read test questions and answer choices at least twice because it's easy to miss something, to transpose a word or some letters. If you have no idea what the correct answer is, skip it and come back later if there's time. If you're still clueless, it's okay to guess. Remember, you're scored on the number of questions you answer correctly and you're not penalized for wrong answers. The worst case scenario is that you miss a point from a good guess.

3. **Turn it on its ear.** The syntax of a question can often provide a clue, so make things interesting and turn the question into a statement to see if it changes the meaning or relates better (or worse) to the answer choices.

4. **Get out your magnifying glass.** Look for hidden clues in the questions because it's difficult to write a multiple-choice question without giving away part of the answer in the options presented. In most questions you can readily eliminate one or two potential answers, increasing your chances of answering correctly to 50/50, which will help out if you've skipped a question and gone back to it (see tip #2).

5. **Call it intuition.** Often your first instinct is correct. If you've been studying the content you've likely absorbed something and have subconsciously retained the knowledge. On questions you're not sure about trust your instincts because a first impression is usually correct.

6. **Graffiti.** Sometimes it's a good idea to mark your answers directly on the test booklet and go back to fill in the optical scan sheet later. You don't get extra points for perfectly blackened ovals. If you choose to manage your test this way, be sure not to mismark your answers when you transcribe to the scan sheet.

7. **Become a clock-watcher.** You have a set amount of time to answer the questions. Don't get bogged down laboring over a question you're not sure about when there are ten others you could answer more readily. If you choose to follow the advice of tip #6, be sure you leave time near the end to go back and fill in the scan sheet.

Do the Drill

No matter how prepared you feel it's sometimes a good idea to apply Murphy's Law. So the following tips might seem silly, mundane, or obvious, but we're including them anyway.

1. **Remember, you are what you eat, so bring a snack.** Choose from the list of energizing foods that appear earlier in the introduction.

2. **You're not too sexy for your test.** Wear comfortable clothes. You'll be distracted if your belt is too tight or if you're too cold or too hot.

3. **Lie to yourself.** Even if you think you're a prompt person, pretend you're not and leave plenty of time to get to the testing center. Map it out ahead of time and do a dry run if you have to. There's no need to add road rage to your list of anxieties.

4. **Bring sharp, number 2 pencils.** It may seem impossible to forget this need from your school days, but you might. And make sure the erasers are intact, too.

5. **No ticket, no test.** Bring your admission ticket as well as **two** forms of identification, including one with a picture and signature. You will not be admitted to the test without these things.

6. **You can't take it with you.** Leave any study aids, dictionaries, note-books, computers, and the like at home. Certain tests **do** allow a scientific or four-function calculator, so check ahead of time to see if your test does.

7. **Prepare for the desert.** Any time spent on a bathroom break **cannot** be made up later, so use your judgment on the amount you eat or drink.

8. **Quiet, Please!** Keeping your own time is a good idea, but not with a timepiece that has a loud ticker. If you use a watch, take it off and place it nearby but not so that it distracts you. And **silence your cell phone**.

To the best of our ability, we have compiled the content you need to know in this book and in the accompanying online resources. The rest is up to you. You can use the study and testing tips or you can follow your own methods. Either way, you can be confident that there aren't any missing pieces of information and there shouldn't be any surprises in the content on the test.

If you have questions about test fees, registration, electronic testing, or other content verification issues please visit *www.ets.org*.

Good luck!

Sharon Wynne
Founder, XAMonline

ABOUT THE PRAXIS EXAMS

PRAXIS Points

1. The PRAXIS Series comprises more than 140 different tests in over seventy different subject areas.

2. Over 90% of the PRAXIS tests measure subject area knowledge.

3. The purpose of the test is to measure whether the teacher candidate possesses a sufficient level of knowledge and skills to perform job duties effectively and responsibly.

4. Your state sets the acceptable passing score.

5. Any candidate, whether from a traditional teaching-preparation path or an alternative route, can seek to enter the teaching profession by taking a PRAXIS test.

6. PRAXIS tests are updated regularly to ensure current content.

ABOUT THE TEST

Praxis tests are designed to measure a teacher's skills, knowledge, and competency in the classroom. They are required by many teaching organizations, and are necessary for licensing and certification purposes. Required Praxis scores vary by state and organization – a school in Florida might have very different standards for Praxis testers than a university in Washington. The details vary, but Praxis remains ubiquitous as a tool to determine a teacher's ability and merit.

The Praxis test is issued at specific testing centers. Some tests are offered all year round, while a few are only offered during specific periods each season. All tests, except Braille Proficiency (0633), are handled via computer. Registration and pay can be handled online, and testing is handled at many universities, Prometric Testing Centers, and other locations. You may need to arrange transportation and time off to get to your nearest testing center. Different states have different registration requirements, but all tests will require a photo ID and printout of your registration ticket. If you fail to achieve your ideal Praxis score, you can retake most tests every 21 days. Accommodations also exist for international teachers, and the disabled. For more details on Praxis requirements by state, visit https://www.ets.org/praxis/states.

The English Language Arts: Content Knowledge (5038) test focuses on the skills English teachers require to instruct in language development, comprehension, and rudiments.

Test Name	English Language Arts: 5038 Content Knowledge
Time allotted	150 minutes
Questions	130 Multiple Choice Questions
Content Categories	Reading, Writing/speaking/Listening, Language Use and Vocabulary

The questions are divided into three equally-sized categories: *Reading; Language Use and Vocabulary; and Writing, Speaking, and Listening. Reading* focuses on English literature, examining the applicant's knowledge of and ability to interpret the dramas, poems, novels, and nonfiction works that make up the English literary canon. *Writing, Speaking, and Listening* focuses on the rhetorical components of writing – writing to inform, to argue, to question, etc. Language Use focuses on the conventions of standard English, such as grammar and syntax.

Categories	Number of Questions	Percentages
Reading	49	38%
Writing, Speaking, Listening	48	37%
Language Use and Vocabulary	33	25%

The following book offers a primer to the knowledge base required to score highly on the Praxis English Language Arts: Content Knowledge exam. English language arts is too broad a subject to tackle in a single document, but this book outlines the essential topics required to pass the Praxis exam and receive your ideal certification.

Interpreting Test Results

Contrary to what you may have heard, the results of a PRAXIS test are not based on time. More accurately, you will be scored on the raw number of points you earn in relation to the raw number of points available. Each question is worth one raw point. It is likely to your benefit to complete as many questions in the time allotted, but it will not necessarily work to your advantage if you hurry through the test.

Follow the guidelines provided by ETS for interpreting your score. The web site offers a sample test score sheet and clearly explains how the scores are scaled and what to expect if you have an essay portion on your test.

Scores are usually available by phone within a month of the test date and scores will be sent to your chosen institution(s) within six weeks. Additionally, ETS now makes online, downloadable reports available for 45 days from the reporting date.

It is **critical** that you be aware of your own state's passing score. Your raw score may qualify you to teach in some states, but not all. ETS administers the test and assigns a score, but the states make their own interpretations and, in some cases, consider combined scores if you are testing in more than one area.

Teaching Trends

Digital pedagogy and the use of 21st century teaching methods have shifted the landscape of teaching to create a bigger focus on student engagement. Student-centered classrooms now utilize technology to create efficiencies and increase digital literacy. Classrooms that once relied on memorization and the regurgitation of facts now push students to create and analyze material. The Blooms Taxonomy chart below gives a great visual of the higher order thinking skills that current teachers are implementing in their learning objectives. There are also examples of the verbs that you might use when creating learning objectives at the assignment, course, or program level.

21st Century Bloom's Taxonomy

Lower-order			Higher-Order		
Remember	Understand	Apply	Analyze	Evaluate	Create
• Define	• Classify	• Determine	• Deduct	• Argue	• Construct
• Describe	• Explain	• Organize	• Estimate	• Justify	• Adapt
• Recall	• Summarize	• Use	• Outline	• Support	• Modify

Most importantly, you'll notice that each of these verbs will allow teachers to align a specific assessment to assess the mastery of the skill that's being taught. Instead of saying "Students will learn about parts of speech," teachers will insert a measurable verb into the learning objective. The 21st century model uses S.M.A.R.T. (Specific, Measurable, Attainable, Realistic, Time-bound) assessment methods to ensure teachers can track progress and zero in on areas that students need to revisit before they have fully grasped the concept.

When reading the first objective below, you might ask yourself the following questions:

Students will:

1. Learn about parts of speech

How will they learn? How will you assess their learning? What does "learn" mean to different teachers? What does "learn" look like to different learning styles?

In this second example, the 21st century model shows specific ways students will use parts of speech.

Students will be able to:

1. Define parts of speech (lower)

2. Classify parts of speech (lower)

3. Construct a visual representation of each part of speech (higher)

Technology in the 21st Century Classroom

Student-centered classrooms now also rely heavily on technology for content delivery (powerpoint, LMS) assessment (online quizzes) and collaborative learning (GoogleDrive). Particular to secondary classrooms, teachers can now record themselves speaking using lecture capture software. Students can then watch the video multiple times to ensure they've understood concepts. They have the ability to pause/rewind/replay any sections they are confused about, and they can focus on taking better notes while having the ability to watch the video a second or third time.

Online assessments also give students and teachers a better idea for comprehension level. These quick, often self-grading assessments give teachers more time to spend with students instead of grading. They eliminate human error and give teachers data needed to zero in on concepts that need to be revisited. For example, if 12 of 15 students got number 5 wrong, the teacher will know to discuss this concept in class. Online assessments may include listening, speaking, reading, and/or writing practice. This reinforces the content that was taught in the classroom and gives opportunity for practice at students' leisure. In addition, adaptable learning will help teachers by tracking user data to demonstrate learning gains. This can be completed in pre-posttest form, with conditionals within an assessment, or through small, formative assessments.

SMART Technologies, Inc. is a very popular company that creates software and hardware for educational environments. You may have heard of a "SmartBoard" before. These are promethean boards (interactive whiteboards) and are most commonly gained using grant money. They can be used as a projector for PowerPoints, their speakers can be used for audio practice, and their video options can allow you to "bring" a guest speaker into your classroom using videoconferencing, such as Skype. They record notes made on the whiteboard and record audio from lectures, which can then be saved and sent to students that were absent, or used to review for tests on varying concepts.

Google has created ample opportunity for secondary teachers in creating efficiencies for document sharing, assessment tools, and collaborative learning environments. Their drive feature can allow for easy transfer of assignment instructions, essays, and group projects. Slides can be used to create and post PowerPoints for students to have ongoing access. Forms is a great way to create quizzes, and the data can be sorted and manipulated in a number of ways. They can also be used for self-assessment, peer evaluation, and for pre-post analyses.

As technology continues to evolve, it's critical for teachers to continue to implement tools that make their classrooms more effective and efficient while also preparing students to successfully function in a technology-driven society. Through simple lessons and technology demonstrations, students will have a great start at applying technology skills in the outside world. The classroom is a great starting place for students to learn how to use technology and how to practice their own reading, writing, listening, and speaking.

SECTION I
READING

SECTION 1
READING

> **SKILL I.A.1** Knows major works and authors of United States, British, World (including non-Western), and young adult literature.
> a. identify the authors and titles of major works of fiction, poetry, drama, and literary nonfiction

Literature

American Literature

Author	Time Period	Contributions & Significant Works
John Winthrop	16th Century	English Puritan lawyer; leading contributor and first governor of the Massachusetts Bay colony *A Model of Christian Charity* *The History of New England*
Anne Bradstreet	17th Century	American Puritan; first woman recognized as an accomplished New World Poet; first female writer in North America to be published *Another* *Another II* *The Prologue* *To My Dear and Loving Husband*
John Edwards	18th Century	Protestant preacher; influential theologian and philosopher "Sinners in the Hands of an Angry God" (sermon) *The End for Which God Created the World* *The Life of David Brainerd* *Religious Affections*

Phillis Wheatley	18th Century	First published African American poet; native to West Africa *Poems on Various Subjects, Religious and Moral*
James Fenimore Cooper	19th Century	Writing influenced by experience working in the US Navy; many of his works referenced life at sea *The Spy* *Leatherstocking Tales*
Frederick Douglass	19th Century	African-American social reformer; escaped slave; leader of abolitionist movement *Narrative of the Life of Frederick Douglass, An American Slave* *My Bondage and My Freedom*
Thomas Jefferson	19th Century	Founding father; former president of the United States; principal author of the Declaration of Independence
Edgar Allen Poe	19th Century	Poet; short story author; Boston native "The Raven" "A Dream Within a Dream"
Abraham Lincoln	19th Century	Former President of the United States; abolished slavery; assassinated Emancipation Proclamation
Nathaniel Hawthorne	19th Century	Dark romance short story author; Salem, MA native *The Scarlet Letter* *Twice-Told Tales* *The House of Seven Gables*
Ralph Waldo Emerson	19th Century	Leader of the transcendentalist movement; poet; essayist; highly influential to the American romantic movement *Essays: First Series* *Essays: Second Series* "Nature" "Uriel" "The Snow-Storm"

Henry David Thoreau	19th Century	Leader of the transcendentalist movement; poet and essayist known for writing about nature and natural history *Walden* "Civil Disobedience"
Walt Whitman	19th Century	Leader in creation of free verse; poet; essayist; journalist; displayed views from transcendentalism and realism; self-published *Leaves of Grass* *Franklin Evans*
Herman Melville	19th Century	Renaissance poet, short story writer, and novelist; spent years at sea before becoming a writer *Typee* *Moby Dick*
Emily Dickinson	19th Century	Prolific Romantic poet; thousands of poems found hidden in her room upon her death *The Complete Poems of Emily Dickinson*
Mark Twain	19th Century	Novelist; known for writing about southern culture *The Adventures of Tom Sawyer* *Adventures of Huckleberry Finn*
Stephen Crane	19th Century	Protestant Methodist poet, short story writer, and novelist; demonstrated realism, naturalism, and impressionism in his works *The Red Badge of Courage* *Maggie: A Girl on the Streets* *War is Kind*
Harriet Beecher Stowe	19th Century	Author of over 30 books; abolitionist; fought for women's rights *Uncle Tom's Cabin*

Kate Chopin	19th Century	Short story and novel writer; known for fiction; accepted to many prestigious magazines *The Awakening*
Henry James	19th Century	Realist; known for narrative fiction *The Portrait of a Lady*
Charlotte Perkins Gilman	19th Century	Novelist; short story writer; poet; feminist; lecturer for social reform "The Yellow Wallpaper"
Gertrude Stein	20th Century	Writer and poet; contributor to the modernist era *Three Lives* *How to Write*
Edith Wharton	20th Century	Novelist; short story writer; Pulitzer Prize winner; known for writing depictions of an affluent lifestyle *The Age of Innocence*
T.S. Eliot	20th Century	Poet; social critic; leader of the Modernist era; Nobel prize winner "The Love Song of J. Alfred Prufrock" *Four Quartets*
William Faulkner	20th Century	Author of novels, short stories, essays, plays, and poetry; Nobel Prize winner; known for incorporating stories about southern culture *As I Lay Dying* *The Sound and the Fury*
Langston Hughes	20th Century	Harlem Renaissance leader; athor of poems and novels; social activist *Let America be America Again* *The Ways of White Folks*

Eugene O'Neill	20th Century	Nobel prize winner; playwright; plays were known for incorporating elements of realism *Beyond the Horizon* *Anna Christie* *Strange Interlude*
Gwendolyn Brooks	20th Century	First African American woman to win the Pulitzer Prize for poetry; Teacher; Poet *Negro Hero* *Annie Allen*
Ernest Hemingway	20th Century	Writer of novels and short stories; Pulitzer Prize winner; Nobel Prize winner *A Farewell to Arms* *The Sun Also Rises* *For Whom the Bell Tolls*
James Baldwin	20th Century	Author of novels, poems, and plays; social justice activist; *Notes of a Native Son*
Toni Morrison	21st Century	Novelist; feminist; Nobel Prize Winner; Pulitzer Prize winner; known for speaking out against racism and sexism *Beloved*
Maya Angelou	21st Century	Poet, Civil Rights Activist *I Know Why the Caged Bird Sings*
Louise Erdrich	21st Century	Novelist; poet; children's book author; known for inclusion of Native American culture *The Plague of Doves*

The earliest literature to come out of North America was produced by the various indigenous tribes that inhabited the continent before European settlers appeared. These stories were almost always oral tellings, passed down from generation to generation, dealing with themes such as the interconnectedness of nature and a reverence for family and tradition. After European colonization began, Native American stories took on a somber tone as they lamented the destruction of their people and culture.

The **Colonial Period** of American literature, by contrast, was written down instead of told orally, and was deeply Christian and neoclassical in style. In the 1630s, the first printing presses were built by colonists in the New World, and they created writings that borrowed heavily from the British literary canon. Colonists were often taught proper English grammar and spelling, and their works depicted the struggles of early colonial life, always with an emphasis on order, family, and religion. William Bradford's Mayflower Compact recounted the daily hardships of colonization during the harsh winter in Massachusetts, whereas Anne Bradstreet explored colonial daily life through poetry. Captain John Smith is sometimes considered the first author of the New World due to his journals recalling his earliest days on the new continent.

Values at this time were distinctly Puritan, emphasizing the church as the center of all daily life. Indeed, much of the writing produced at this time was intended simply to be read aloud during sermons. It wasn't until the **Revolutionary Period** in the mid-1700s that works of a more political nature began to appear.

In 1775, Thomas Paine, a philosopher and activist, wrote a pamphlet that would become the top-selling piece of American literature of all time. *Common Sense* was an incendiary piece of writing, detailing in clear, simple prose the need for rebellion against British rule. The pamphlet's fierce rhetoric stirred the hearts of the colonial upper class, and its concise style meant it could be read aloud in taverns and town squares so that even the illiterate could hear Paine's words. John Adams would later say, "Without the pen of the author of *Common Sense*, the sword of Washington would have been raised in vain." *Common Sense* epitomized this period of American literature, emphasizing freedom from Britain and the need to forge a new identity as Americans.

Among the educated elite, enlightenment was the watchword of the day. Enlightenment thinkers criticized the religious and political dogma they had been raised with, insisting that a new social order based on reason was necessary to modernize the human race. Some enlightenment thinkers, like Benjamin Franklin, explored new concepts of morality outside of Puritanism – Franklin's *Poor Richard's Almanack* was a collection of wit and wisdom that detailed Franklin's concepts of common virtue in an entertaining style. Many of Franklin's aphorisms from this book ("A penny saved is a penny earned") survive to this day.

The Revolutionary Period also produced stirring oration – Patrick Henry's "Speech to the Virginia House of Burgesses" produced the timeless quotation "Give me liberty or give me death!" This directness was a necessary component of Revolutionary writing, as it needed to be accessible to even the uneducated and illiterate citizens the upper class wished to recruit.

Even the Declaration of Independence exhibits characteristics of good Revolutionary literature. Written by Thomas Jefferson, it offers neoclassical style, direct prose, and plenty of irresistible quotations that deliver a unified political message.

The 1800s saw the rise of the **Romantic Period** in American literature. Romanticism was considered very liberal and radical for its time, a reaction to the Industrial Revolution and the increasing scientific rationalization of nature. Romanticism focused on intense emotions, such as awe, horror, love, lust, and depression, and found artistic beauty in the wonders of nature. American Romanticists also lionized their own exploits – the trials against the Indians, Manifest Destiny, and the triumphs of Revolutionary heroes like George Washington. Later critics would characterize Romanticism as naïve, but the influence of the movement on world literature was indelible.

Washington Irving was an early American Romantic, creating folk tales like "The Legend of Sleepy Hollow" and "Rip Van Winkle," which largely rejected British influence in favor of a new American consciousness. The Romantic Period also saw a rise in poetry intended to be read as cozy fireside entertainment. "Fireside Poets" such as James Russell Lowell, Oliver Wendell Holmes, and John Greenleaf Whittier wrote of scenarios familiar to Americans at the time, such as the harshness and beauty of New England winters. Henry Wadsworth Longfellow wrote longer poetic epics like *The Song of Hiawatha* and *The Courtship of Miles Standish* which could thrill as well as educate.

Another prominent American Romantic author is Edgar Allan Poe. Among the first authors to make his living solely by writing, Poe's influence has been felt around the world. With short stories like "Murders in the Rue Morgue," Poe invented the genre of detective fiction, and works like "The Cask of Amontillado" pioneered in the genre of horror. His works explored topics of depression and family strife, drawing heavily upon his own struggles. He had a major influence on other genres like science fiction and mystery, and he is considered one of the all-time masters of the short story, helping to establish it as a major literary form.

Meanwhile, Nathaniel Hawthorne offered some of the first true criticisms of the Puritan lifestyle that had been so prominent in Colonial times. *The Scarlet Letter* is considered his masterwork, depicting the public shaming and ostracization of Hester Prynne, a Puritan woman accused of adultery. Though a fundamentally Romantic book, it eschews much of the wide-eyed naiveté common to the movement, focusing more on the grim realities of human nature.

This political bent in Romantic literature was pushed further by the "Transcendentalists" – Henry David Thoreau and Ralph Waldo Emerson created this subgenre of Romanticism which sought beauty in the simplicity of nature and freedom from the struggles of society. Both authors were intensely political and anti-government, this being reflected in the works *Walden* and the anti-authoritarian screed "On the Duty of Civil Disobedience." In *Walden*, Thoreau painted an attractive portrait of his time living simply in the bounty of nature. The book mixes social commentary, satire, and observations of the natural world to great effect.

But perhaps the single most prominent work of American Romantic literature is Herman Melville's *Moby Dick*. The timeless story pits mad Captain Ahab against the whale that took his leg, casting their struggle as a battle between man and nature, or perhaps man against the very universe itself. Melville explores a heightened dialect in the book, harkening back to the works of Shakespeare or the ancient Greeks, which rejects realism in favor of operatic emotion. Though unappreciated in its time, the story is now considered among the best novels ever produced by an American.

As the Romantic Period faded in the 1850s with the American Civil War, a new **Realist Period** began to take hold. Americans felt Romantic writings no longer reflected the grim realities of life during wartime and began producing simpler, more grounded literature, replete with imagery and often expressing cynicism and dissatisfaction.

Walt Whitman was among the early Realist pioneers. His poetry made use of simple images and was very prose-like. He's considered the "Father of Free Verse" for his influential style, which shirked much of the established rules of poetry of the time. Emily Dickinson is also sometimes considered a Realist. A reclusive woman, Dickinson's body of work is deeply introspective, focusing on intense sensory input and attention to detail that reflects her apprehension of the outside world.

But no one captured the sentiment of post-Civil War America quite like Mark Twain. The pen name of Samuel Longhorn Clemens, Twain is considered by many to be America's first great humorist, penning works of staggering wit that oozed nostalgia, appealing to both young readers and old. His works explore the American South during the Reconstruction period, drawing on his own childhood and adventures as a river boat worker for inspiration. His works, like *The Adventures of Huckleberry Finn*, also explore racial themes and are considered controversial to this day.

Other authors of note include Stephen Crane, whose book, *The Red Badge of Courage*, offered a realistic depiction of a soldier's life during the Civil War. He also wrote *Maggie: A Girl of the Streets,* a cynical tale of a poor woman who turns to prostitution. Upton Sinclair's work is similarly unromantic, with books like *The Jungle* exposing the deplorable working conditions of Chicago meat packers. Sinclair was considered a major agitator in his time. He also wrote *Oil!*, which criticized the greed of American oilmen and proved extremely controversial due to its depiction of a sexual encounter in a motel.

Twentieth Century literature is very diverse due to the rise of mass media, and can be divided into the realms of fiction, poetry, and drama. Among the greatest American dramatists is Eugene O'Neill, who won an unprecedented four Pulitzer Prizes ford drama for his works. Deeply personal, O'Neill's works reflect his own struggles with depression, alcoholism, and family dysfunction that bordered on abuse. His masterpiece is *A Long Day's Journey Into Night*, a semi-autobiographical tale of a family being slowly torn apart by substance abuse and their own incompatible egos. Tennessee Williams is another giant of American drama, penning classics like *Cat On a Hot Tin Roof* and *A Streetcar Named Desire*, which deal with issues of sexuality, gender, and mental illness. Both dramatists evoked the Realist style from decades earlier, creating terse and sometimes pessimistic deconstructions of modern American life through the lenses of volatile families and failed careers.

In poetry, the 20th century produced such great names as T.S. Eliot, Hart Crane, Robert Frost, and Wallace Stevens. Other popular poets include Maya Angelou and Langston Hughes. Angelou was a civil rights activist who wrote poetry and memoirs on themes of racism and gender, with the autobiographical *I Know Why the Caged Bird Sings* detailing her growth from an insecure and abused young woman into an independent firebrand. Hughes, likewise, wrote detailed accounts of the African-American experience. He was a leading figure in the Harlem Renaissance, a move-ment in the 1920s that gave voice to black writers in New York City, many of whom would go on to become quite influential. Frost's poems are more traditional, detailing the beauty of the natural world he experienced growing up in rural New England. His poem "The Road Less Traveled" is among the most well-known and acclaimed work of our time.

But prose fiction has always had the largest reach and greatest influence, and many 20th century American authors have written works that continue to change the world. In 1925, F. Scott Fitzgerald published *The Great Gatsby*, considered by many to be among the greatest American novels. The book follows wealthy, newly rich Jay Gatsby as viewed through the eyes of his friend and confidante Nick Carraway. Gatsby tries in vain to leverage his vast wealth and influence and win the woman of his dreams. The book exposes the vacuity of the wealth and material gains that so many Americans strive for.

John Steinbeck explored the struggles of the economically deprived. Steinbeck's *The Grapes of Wrath* follows the Joad family during the Great Depression as they try time and again to carve out a better future for themselves, being twarted at every turn by greedy opportunists and exploitative businessmen. Steinbeck wrote in a very collo-quial dialect that made his works extremely popular.

Hemingway developed a new style involving simple words and short declarative sentences that emphasized action and image rather than introspection. He wrote philosophical tales of fate like *The Old Man and the Sea* and wartime narratives like *A Farewell to Arms* and *For Whom the Bell Tolls*.

And lastly, William Faulkner explored sometimes grotesque scenarios involving characters in the American South. Faulkner's work described the lingering effects of slavery and the erosion of traditional Southern institutions in an absurdist and experimental style. *As I Lay Dying* and *The Sound and the Fury* are considered his masterpieces.

Since the beginning, American literature has focused largely on issues of class, race, religion, and the struggle for independence, be it from oppressive institutions, economic inequality, or bigotry. The so-called "pioneer spirit" can still be found in contemporary American iconography. The cowboys and superheroes that Americans enjoy reflect a fierce belief in the power of the individual and the need to struggle against life's unfairness. Much world literature focuses on groups, on collectives or movements, but it is not uncommon for American stories to focus on one character only and tell a more universal tale through that character's experiences. From the earliest pioneer tales to modern stories of the empty promises of the American Dream, the United States has proved itself a powerhouse in the world of literature.

British Literature

Author	Time Period	Significant Works & Contributions
Unknown	~700-1000 AD	Old English epic poem from the Anglo-Saxon period; the exact date is unknown, and the author is also a mystery; arguably the oldest poem ever written in Old English "Beowulf"
The Gawain poet / Unknown	14th Century	Poems written in Middle English; author unknown; *Pearl* *Sir Gawain and the Green Knight*
Geoffrey Chaucer	15th Century	Poet; known as the "Father of English literature"; arguably the best poet of the Middle Ages *The Canterbury Tales*

Sir Thomas Malory	15th Century	Knight; author of the first prose piece in English *Le Morte d'Arthur*
William Shakespeare	17th Century	Arguably the best poet and dramatist of all time; known for wit and tragedy *Sonnets* *Hamlet* *Romeo and Juliet* *A Midsummer Night's Dream*
John Donne	17th Century	Poet; known for love poems, religious poems, and sonnets "An Anatomy of the World"
John Milton	17th Century	Poet; best known for writing in blank verse *Paradise Lost*
Samuel Johnson	18th Century	Poet; essayist; literary critic; known for being a devout Anglican; influencer of Modern English *A Dictionary of the English Language*
Alexander Pope	18th Century	Poet; known for satirical writing style *Essay on Criticism* *The Rape of the Lock*
Johnathan Swift	18th Century	Poet; essayist; Anglo-Irish; known as master of satire *Gulliver's Travels*
William Blake	19th Century	Poet; contributor to the Romantic Age *Songs of Innocence* *Milton*
William Wordsworth	19th Century	Poet; leader of the Romantic Movement *Lyrical Ballads*
Samuel Taylor Coleridge	19th Century	Poet; leader of the Romantic Movement *The Rime of the Ancient Mariner*

Jane Austen	19th Century	Best known for writing about women's roles in affluent English communities *Sense and Sensibility* *Pride and Prejudice*
Percy Shelley	19th Century	Romantic poet; husband of Mary Shelley; known for radical content *Ode to the West Wind*
Mary Wollstonecraft	18th Century	Women's rights activist; feminist *A Vindication of the Rights of Woman*
Lord Byron	19th Century	Poet; leader of the Romantic Movement *Don Juan*
John Keats	19th Century	Romantic poet; known for imagery and odes "Ode to a Nightingale"
Charles Dickens	19th Century	Fiction writer; arguably the best author of the Victorian Era *Oliver Twist* *Great Expectations* *A Tale of Two Cities*
Emily Brontë	19th Century	Teacher, poet, and novelist; contributor to the Victorian Era *Wuthering Heights*
Charlotte Brontë	19th Century	Oldest Brontë sister; novelist and poet; contributor to the Victorian Era *Jane Eyre*
Matthew Arnold	19th Century	Victorian poet; known for highly intellectual writing "Dover Beach"

William Butler Yeats	20th Century	Poet; Nobel Prize winner; arguably one of the best poets in the 20th Century; known for lyrical poetry; Protestant; Anglo-Irish *The Green Helmet and Other Poems*
James Joyce	20th Century	Irish novelist and poet; highly influential author in the 20th Century *Dubliners* *A Portrait of the Artist as a Young Man*
George Bernard Shaw	20th Century	Playwright; Anglo-Irish; Nobel Prize winner *Man and Superman* *Pygmalion*
Virginia Woolf	20th Century	Author and journalist; leader of Modernist Era *Mrs. Dalloway* *To the Lighthouse*
Dylan Thomas	20th Century	Welsh poet; known for erratic writing "Do not go gentle into that good night"
Doris Lessing	21st Century	Poet, novelist, and short story writer; Nobel Prize winner; feminist *The Golden Notebook*
Seamus Heaney	21st Century	Irish poet and playwright; Nobel Prize winner; known for describing the struggle of living in Northern Ireland as a Catholic *Wintering Out*

The myriad varieties of literature found throughout the world are too numerous to explore in any one book, but for the purposes of AP study, some of the most significant literary accomplishments can be summarized. Remember, there is no substitute for in-depth research. Read reviews, summaries, criticisms, or the works themselves to get a fuller understanding of the power these stories have held in whatever culture they have their roots. The most significant direct influence on American literature comes from our neighbors across the Atlantic in the British Isles. During the Anglo-Saxon period between the 8th and 11th centuries, the English language was still coming into its own as a unique dialect separate from Latin or German. Among the earliest works in the English language is *Beowulf*, an epic poem describing the exploits of its titular hero as he attempts to slay the monstrous creature, Grendel. *Beowulf*'s author is not known. The story likely originated as an oral telling that distorted real historical events into the realm of myth.

The medieval period lasted until the 15th century and introduced many other stories that have become an essential part of British consciousness. Thomas Malory's *La Morte D'Arthur* recounts one of the first Arthurian legends, describing the exploits of King Arthur, Guinevere, Sir Lancelot, and the rest of the Knights of the Round Table, thus making an indelible mark on world literature. But Geoffrey Chaucer's *Canterbury Tales* is the true apex of Medieval British literature. This work, which follows a group of pilgrims engaged in a storytelling contest as they travel to a famous shrine, featured an unprecedented mastery of common language and a large cast of characters from all walks of life. Chaucer introduced many new words and phrases into the English language. His view of English life as seen through the eyes of worldly lower class laborers has proven invaluable to historians ever since.

Of course, no mention of British literature is complete without Shakespeare and his contemporaries who worked during the **Renaissance Era** of the 14th through 17th centuries. Considered by many to be the greatest writer in the English language, William Shakespeare produced thirty-nine plays – ranging from broad comedies to heartfelt tragedies and bloody historical tellings – and over one hundred sonnets. Shakespeare was a master of iambic pentameter, a poetical meter in which each line five iambs or "feet," each containing a stressed and unstressed syllable. This style of verse was said to mimic the beating of the human heart, and it lent Shakespeare's prose a lively energy that has proved attractive to actors and readers for centuries. Shakespeare was a great wit and an incredible craftsman of language. No other author has contributed more words to the English language than Shakespeare. His contemporaries, such as Christopher Marlowe and John Webster, also experimented with new forms of vernacular storytelling.

In the 17th century, British literature largely focused on religious concerns. John Milton, a staunch Puritan, gave *Paradise Lost* to the world. This epic poem details the fall of the archangel Lucifer from heaven and his rebellion against God. The work proved so influential that it is sometimes mistaken for Biblical canon. John Bunyan's *The Pilgrim's Progress* is also staunchly religious, telling of a man's journey towards heaven after death. For many years, the book was second only to the Bible in terms of sales. John Donne's poetry, meanwhile, was more personal and introspective. Common turns of phrase like "for whom the bell tolls" and "no man is an island" come from his works.

18th century British literature became even more intensely political following the revival of the monarchy under Charles II. **Neoclassical** writing was the rule at this time, as British citizens sought to reconnect with their past. Notable authors include Alexander Pope, a poet who dabbled in a variety of neoclassical forms, and Robert Burns, a Scotsman who explored common Scottish brogue in his poems such as "To A Mouse." But William Blake came to be viewed as the preeminent voice of this generation. A notably progressive thinker with decidedly anti-church politics, Blake fought for the dissolution of gender roles and more critical views of religion. He was also a poet of mystical insight. He was a contemporary of Thomas Paine, and the two shared many views popular amongst Enlightenment figures at this time.

The works of Blake help usher in an era of **Romanticism** in British literature in the 1800s. The "first generation" of Romantics included William Wordsworth and Samuel Taylor Coleridge, who collaborated to publish *Lyrical Ballads*, a collection of experimental poems like "Rime of the Ancient Mariner" that epitomized the Romantic style. The poems in this collection also illustrated Wordsworth's philosophical belief that men are inherently good but can be corrupted by society.

The Second Generation of Romantics includes John Keats, Lord Byron, and Percy Bysshe Shelley, who wrote sonnets and narrative poems. Byron's *Don Juan* is a masterpiece of British satire, and his autobiographical *Childe Harold's Pilgrimage* is exceedingly self-deprecating. Shelley's works feature remarkable sensory detail. His poem "Ozymandias" describes a traveler who discovers a monument to a forgotten pharoah whose grand empire has crumbled to dust. Keats' works display maturity far beyond his years, as the poet died at the early age of 25.

The Romantic era also saw the rise of the some of the first prominent female authors in British history, creating a feminist perspective that was often missing from literature until that point. Jane Austen is the most popular author from this time, and her works, such as *Pride & Prejudice* and *Mansfield Park*, embody realistic characters and social commentary that have endured in popularity even to the present day. Charlotte and Emily Brontë were sisters and professional rivals, who wrote *Jane Eyre* and *Wuthering Heights* respectively, two grand Romantic novels focusing on duplicity and unrequited love amongst the landed gentry of England. All of these authors struggled against societal expectations of women during this time, and many critics were less than generous with their reviews, leading another prominent author of this time,

Mary Ann Evans, to write under the alias of George Eliot to get a fairer appraisal of her work.

The rise of print media in the 1800s created a diverse range of literature in Britain, ranging from the sharply **satirical** to the proudly **adventurous**. Great satirists like Oscar Wilde skewered the manners and customs of the upper class to a greater degree than ever before, earning scorn from censors and traditionalists while keeping readers enraptured. It was also a great time for young adult literature. Robert Louis Stevenson's *Treasure Island* wove an action-packed tale of high adventure that appealed to young readers. Still other authors focused their attention on social commentary, such as Rudyard Kipling, who created many fables and parables that taught valuable lessons in works such as *The Jungle Book*. Charles Dickens's works were more critical, deconstructing Victorian values of greed and decadence, focusing attention on the downtrodden orphans and lower class laborers who suffered during the Industrial Revolution. He also wrote immensely popular stories such as *A Christmas Carol*, which helped re-popularize the Christmas holiday and has never once been out of publication since its first printing.

This experimentation and variety has continued in the 20th century, in which Britain has firmly established itself as a major force in world literature. Irish authors James Joyce and Samuel Beckett pioneered **Modernist** literature, which remixed and recontextualized existing dramatic forms in absurd, experimental new ways. Beckett's *Waiting for Godot* is among the most influential plays ever written, examining the tragedy and comedy of the human condition via two clownish vagabonds contemplating their own inability to accomplish anything of note. The play is a landmark work of Absurdist and Post-Modern theater, two experimental styles that pushed the limits of what audiences could expect from the stage.

Joyce's *Ulysses* is considered by many critics to be among the greatest novels in the English language. It experiments and invents in nearly every literary style, using the dreamlike stream-of-consciousness narrative of a man's madcap journey through Dublin on a single day.

The works of George Orwell are more political. A former police officer in English-occupied Burma, Orwell wrote works that are fiercely anti-fascist, providing stark warnings about the dangers of totalitarianism. His science-fiction/dystopian novel *1984* is considered his masterpiece, telling the tale of a common man's struggle against a brutally conformist society led by the mysterious dictator, "Big Brother."

British literature has flitted between proud lionization of their own accomplishments and self-deprecating laughter at their failings. Traditions of satire and wordplay run deep in English writings, from the comedies of Shakespeare with their puns and double entendres, to the biting, controversial ironies of Oscar Wilde. Still other authors have sought to elevate institutions of British life, such as religion or the monarchy. British writings owe a strong debt to the works of the ancient Greeks, whose tragedies and philosophical writings inspired countless English-language works. The body of work produced by this small island nations continues to grow and develop, further establishing its place as a force to be reckoned with in world media.

World Literature

Author	Time Period	Significant Works & Contributions
Michel de Montaigne	16th Century	French philosopher and essayist *Essais*
Miguel de Cervantes Saavedra	16th Century	Spanish novelist, poet, and playwright; arguably the best author in the Spanish language *Don Quixote*
Molière	17th Century	French playwright and actor; known for comedic roles *The Misanthrope*
Jean-Jacques Rousseau	18th Century	Philosopher, author, and composer; said to have influenced the enlightenment *Emile, or On Education*
Johann Wolfgang von Goethe	19th Century	German writer and poet *The Sorrows of Young Werther*
Leo Tolstoy	20th Century	Russian author; arguably one of the greatest writers of all time *War and Peace* *Anna Karenina*
Anton Chekhov	20th Century	Russian M.D., short story writer, and playwright; arguably one of the best fiction writers of all time *The Cherry Orchard*
Franz Kafka	20th Century	German novelist and short story writer; highly influential on 20th century literature *Amerika*

Isak Dinesen	20th Century	Danish author; best known for supernatural topics *Out of Africa*
Jorge Luis Borges	20th Century	Short-story writer, essayist, and poet; native of Argentina *Ficciones* *El Aleph*
Primo Levi	20th Century	Short story writer, novelist, and poet; Holocaust survivor; native of Italy *If This Is a Man*
Yehuda Amichai	20th Century	Israeli Modern poet "And this is Your Glory"
Nadine Gordimer	20th Century	South African author; Nobel Prize winner; political activist; humanitarian *No Time Like the Present*
Pablo Neruda	20th Century	Chilean poet; diplomat *Twenty Love Poems and a Song of Despair*
Czeslaw Milosz	21st Century	Polish poet, diplomat, and professor; known for incorporating naïve concepts about culture and war *The World*
Wole Soyinka	21st Century	Nigerian poet and playwright; Nobel Prize winner; most recently vowed to leave the U.S. due to election of Donald Trump *The Man Died: Prison Notes*
R. K. Narayan	21st Century	Indian author; known for writing about humor and compassion *The Guide*
Margaret Atwood	21st Century	Canadian author; environmental activist *Unearthing Suite*
Derek Walcott	21st Century	St. Lucian professor, poet, and playwright; Nobel Prize winner *Dream on Monkey Mountain*

Naguib Mahfouz	21st Century	Egyptian contemporary writer; existentialist; Nobel Prize winner *The Cairo Trilogy*
Ōe Kenzaburō	21st Century	Japanese contemporary writer; known for incorporating sexual metaphors; Nobel Prize winner *Shiiku*
V. S. Naipaul	21st Century	Native of Trinidad; known for writing about comedy and life in the Caribbean; Nobel Prize winner *A House for Mr. Biswas*

The Praxis English test focuses largely on American and British writings, but a familiarity with other figures of world literature is also useful.

Among the most important authors from the rest of the European continent, **ancient Greek** dramatists such as Sophocles, Euripedes, and Aeschylus wrote many tragedies that have formed the backbone of much of Western literature. Greek tragedies focus largely on the failings of the main character, on their pride (or "hubris") that causes them to subvert the natural order of things and earn the ire of the gods. These things eventually lead to their downfall (a "catharsis" or cleansing). Most of their plays contain a mythic or religious component, and many end with direct intervention from the gods themselves (termed a "deus ex machina," a sudden ending where a godlike figure appears and re-establishes order). Important Greek tragedies include *Oedipus Rex, Medea*, and *Antigone.*

The epics of Homer are also noteworthy, standing, as they do, at the very head of the Western tradition. Two works are attributed to Homer, *The Iliad* and *The Odyssey*, epic poems that describe the exploits of Greek warriors and their struggles against each other and the gods themselves. Homer is the first great European author, and his influence cannot be overstated.

French literature has also proven very influential to American writers. Victor Hugo is considered to be one of the most important French authors, penning heartbreaking novels like *The Hunchback of Notre Dame* and *Les Miserables*. These two books explore the suffering of outcasts and the lower class, in a manner similar to that Charles Dickens across the English Channel. The works of Alexandre Dumas are more pulpy and readable, often classified as swashbucklers or tales of high adventure. Dumas' works include *The Three Musketeers* and *The Count of Monte Cristo,* focusing on tales of revenge, rebellion, and complex love triangles. His works have been translated into over 100 languages and have formed the basis for countless adaptations into film and theater.

One of the most important writers from the **Slavic** nations (he wrote, however, in German) would have to be Franz Kafka. Though largely unnoticed during his lifetime, Kafka is now considered one of the most influential figures in 20th century literature, writing accounts of depression, anxiety, and isolation that blended the realistic and surreal. He was among the first authors to criticize bureaucratic institutions, with works like *The Trial* and *In the Penal Colony*, which feature characters being tormented by shadowy government figures for reasons that are never fully explained. He also delved into more fantastical subject matter with works like *The Metamorphosis*, a tale of a traveling salesman who awakens one day to find he has been transformed into a massive bug. The term "Kafkaesque" is common in literary criticism today, describing situations in which a main character is being persecuted for unclear reasons and has no clear method of escaping his terrible situation.

Russian literary greats include Leo Tolstoy, who described Napolean's capture of the city of Moscow in *War and Peace*, and Fyodor Dostoyevski, who wrote *The Brothers Karamazov*, a philosophical depiction of the dissolving relationship between three brothers and their father that eventually culminates in murder. Tolstoy wrote *Anna Karenina*, a prime example of Realist fiction that follows the exploits of its titular heroine as she pursues a doomed affair with a wealthy count. The 20th century gave Vladimir Nabokov to the world, the controversial author of such works as *Lolita*, which describes the relationship between a literarily-minded pedophile and his stepdaughter. Nabokov's works are replete with sensory detail and are sharply ironic, offering many cutting observations about the American culture that Nabokov gradually assimilated into.

Anton Chekov is considered Russia's prime dramatist, giving the world plays like *Uncle Vanya* and *The Cherry Orchard* that stretched the limits of actors' abilities and paved new ground for concepts like subtext and psychological realism in theater.

These works form much of the basis for the Western canon of literature. One can study them for a lifetime and not scratch the surface of the stories available. For the purposes of the Praxis exam, however, and a functional understanding of Western literature, a good comprehension of the primary titles and authors will suffice.

SKILL I.A.2 **Knows the historical, cultural, and literary contexts of major works and authors of United States, British, and World literature.**
a. identify the historical or literary context of major works of fiction, poetry, drama, and literary nonfiction

See skill I.A.1.

SKILL I.A.3 **Understands the defining characteristics of primary literary genres.**
a. identify typical characteristics of a genre
b. apply correct terminology for a genre (e.g., stanza versus paragraph)

Poetry Versus Prose

Poetry follows a structure with metric or rhyme scheme, while prose does not have a standard style of writing. In addition, poetry often leads the reader to read between the lines, while prose invites a much more literal approach. There is minimal critical thinking involved when it comes to reading a piece of prose. You are simply reading a story. You usually do not have to continuously question the author's intention or the intended meaning of the piece.

Poetry	Prose
Written in verse	Written in narrative form
Contains poetic meter	Contains paragraphs
Reader determines author's intention	Includes a setting, characters, plot, and a point of view
Metaphorical	Literal

If you were to write a piece in both poetry and prose formats and put them beside one another, they would represent the same idea using extremely different formats. Take a look at the two examples below, Emily Dickinson's famous poem "*The Carriage*," and "*Life*" by Charlotte Brontë.

Example 1: *The Carriage*
Poetry

Because I could not stop for Death –
He kindly stopped for me –
The Carriage held but just Ourselves –
And Immortality.

We slowly drove – He knew no haste
And I had put away
My labor and my leisure too,
For His Civility –

We passed the School, where Children strove
At Recess – in the Ring –
We passed the Fields of Gazing Grain –
We passed the Setting Sun –

Or rather – He passed us –
The Dews drew quivering and chill –
For only Gossamer, my Gown –
My Tippet – only Tulle –

We paused before a House that seemed
A Swelling of the Ground –
The Roof was scarcely visible –
The Cornice – in the Ground –

Since then – 'tis Centuries – and yet
Feels shorter than the Day
I first surmised the Horses' Heads
Were toward Eternity –
                    —*Emily Dickinson*

Prose version

As I look back on my life, I cannot help but think about lost opportunity and what it will be like when I leave this world. (She dies and is buried in a cemetery where she will stay for eternity.)

Example 2: *Life*
Poetry

Life, believe, is not a dream
So dark as sages say;
Oft a little morning rain
Foretells a pleasant day.
Sometimes there are clouds of gloom,
But these are transient all;
If the shower will make the roses bloom,
O why lament its fall?

Rapidly, merrily,
Life's sunny hours flit by,
Gratefully, cheerily,
Enjoy them as they fly!

What though Death at times steps in
And calls our Best away?
What though sorrow seems to win,
O'er hope, a heavy sway?
Yet hope again elastic springs,
Unconquered, though she fell;
Still buoyant are her golden wings,
Still strong to bear us well.
Manfully, fearlessly,

The day of trial bear,
For gloriously, victoriously,
Can courage quell despair!
                            —*Charlotte Brontë*

Prose version

I think it's critical to understand that even if you're having a bad day, your outlook and attitude can help you be happy. Everyone should strive to live life in the moment and enjoy the good times because time passes by faster than you'd expect.

Prose Categories

Fictional prose: The most common example of fictional prose is a novel. Using a narrative form of writing, fictional prose has been used to tell tales of adventure, erotica, and mystery. Other examples include romance and short story.

Nonfiction prose: Nonfiction prose is based on facts, but it may also include fictional elements. It is used to be informative and persuasive, yet it does not include any scientific evidence to support its claims. Examples include: journal entry, biography, and essay.

Heroic prose: Also written in the narrative form, heroic prose has a dramatic style that allows for the works to be recited or performed. The most common form of heroic prose is the legend.

Rhymed prose: The difference between prose and poetry is not always clear. Rhymed prose is written with rhymes that are not metrical and is considered to be an artistic, skilled form of writing across the world. Examples include Rayok in Russian culture, Saj' from Arabic culture, and Fu from Chinese culture.

Prose poetry: Prose poetry can be considered a combination, or fusion, of both poetry and prose. It uses extreme imagery, yet does not include the typical metrical structure or rhyme scheme found in a poem.

Types of Prose

Allegory: A story in verse or prose with characters representing virtues and vices. An allegory has two meanings: symbolic and literal. John Bunyan's The Pilgrim's Progress is the most renowned of this genre.

Epistle: A letter that was not always intended for public distribution, but due to the fame of the sender and/or recipient, becomes widely known. Paul wrote epistles that were later placed in the Bible.

Essay: Typically a relatively short prose work focusing on a topic, propounding a definite point of view and using an authoritative tone. Great essayists include Carlyle, Lamb, DeQuincy, Emerson, and Montaigne (who is credited with defining this genre).

Legend: A traditional narrative or collection of related narratives, popularly regarded as historically factual but actually a mixture of fact and fiction. The tales of King Arthur or Robin Hood could be described as legends.

Novel: The longest form of fictional prose containing a variety of characters, settings, local color, and regionalism. Most novels have complex plots, expanded descriptions, and attention to detail. Some of the great novelists include Jane Austen, the Brontë sisters, Twain, Tolstoy, Hugo, Hardy, Dickens, Hawthorne, Forster, and Flaubert.

Romance: A highly imaginative tale set in a fantastical realm dealing with the conflicts between heroes, villains, and/or monsters. "The Knight's Tale" from Chaucer's Canterbury Tales, Sir Gawain and the Green Knight, and Keats' "The Eve of St. Agnes" are representatives.

Short story: Typically a terse narrative, with less development and background about characters; may include description, author's point of view, and tone. Poe emphasized that a successful short story should create one focused impact. Some great short story writers are Hemingway, Faulkner, Twain, Joyce, Shirley Jackson, Flannery O'Connor, Guy de Maupassant, Saki, Edgar Allen Poe, and Pushkin.

Analyzing Prose

The analysis of prose, similar to the analysis of poetry, calls attention to structural elements so as to discern meaning, purpose, and themes. The author's intentions are gleaned through the elements he or she uses and how they are used. Because your written response questions will most likely include either poetry or prose within the prompt, it's critical to deeply analyze all structural elements (plot, characters, setting, and point of view). This will assist you in supporting your own claims and will give you the best opportunity for a high score on the writing portion.

Plot:

The plot is the sequence of events (it may or may not be chronological) that the author chooses to represent the story to be told-both the underlying story and the externals of the occurrences the author relates. An author may use "flashbacks" to tell the back story (or what went before the current events begin). Often, authors begin their stories *in medias res,* or in the middle of things, and, over time, supply the details of what has gone before to provide a clearer picture to the reader of all the relevant events.

Sometimes authors tell parallel stories in order to make their points. For example, in Leo Tolstoy's classic *Anna Karenina*, the unhappy extramarital affair of Anna Karenina and Count Vronsky is contrasted with the happy marriage of Lev and Kitty through the use of alternating chapters devoted to each couple. The plot consists of the progress of each couple: Anna and Count Vronsky into deeper neurosis, obsession, and emotional pain, and Lev and Kitty into deeper and more meaningful partnership through growing emotional intimacy, parenthood, and caring for members of their extended family.

In good novels, each part of the plot is necessary and has a purpose. For example, in *Anna Karenina*, a chapter is devoted to a horse race in which Count Vronsky participates. This might seem like mere entertainment, but, in fact, Count Vronsky is riding his favorite mare, and, in a moment of carelessness in taking a jump, puts the whole weight of his body on the mare's back, breaking it. The horse must be shot. Vronsky loved and admired the mare, but being overcome by a desire to win, he kills the very thing he loves. Similarly, Anna descends into obsession and jealousy as their affair isolates her from society and separates her from her child. Ultimately she kills herself. The chapter symbolizes the destructive effect that Vronsky's love, coupled with inordinate desire, has upon what and whom he loves.

Other authors use repetitious plot lines to reveal the larger story over time. For example, in Joseph Heller's tragic-comedy *Catch-22*, the novel repeatedly returns to a horrific incident in an airplane while it was flying a combat mission. Each time the protagonist, Yossarian, recalls the incident, more detail is revealed. The reader knows from the beginning that this incident is key to why Yossarian wants to be discharged from the army, but it is not until the full details of the gruesome incidents are revealed late in the book that the reader knows why the incident has driven Yossarian almost mad. Interspersed with comedic and ironic episodes, the book's climax (the full revealing of the incident) remains powerfully with the reader, showing the absurdity, insanity, and inhumanity of war. The comic device of Catch-22, a fictitious army rule from which the title is derived, makes this point in a funny way: Catch-22 states that a soldier cannot be discharged from the army unless he is crazy; yet, if he wants to be discharged from the army, he is not crazy. This rule seems to embody the insanity, absurdity, and inhumanity of war.

Characters:

Characters usually represent or embody an idea or ideal acting in the world. For example, in the *Harry Potter* series, Harry Potter's goodness, courage and unselfishness as well as his capacity for friendship and love make him a powerful opponent to Voldemort, whose selfishness, cruelty, and isolation make him the leader of the evil forces in the epic battle of good versus evil. Memorable characters are many-sided: Harry is not only brave, strong, and true, he is vulnerable and sympathetic; orphaned as a child, bespectacled, and often misunderstood by his peers, Harry is not a stereotypical hero.

Charles Dickens's *Oliver Twist* illustrates the principle of goodness, oppressed and unrecognized, unleashed in a troubled world. Oliver encounters a great deal of evil, which he refuses to cooperate with, and also a great deal of good in people who have sympathy for his plight. In contrast to the gentle, kindly, and selfless Maylies who take Oliver in, recognizing his goodness, are the evil Bill Sykes and Fagin—thieves and murderers—who are willing to sell and hurt others for their own gain. When Nancy, a thief in league with Sykes and Fagin, essentially "sells" herself to help Oliver, she represents redemption from evil through sacrifice.

Setting:

The setting of a work of fiction adds a great deal to the story. Historical fiction relies firmly on an established time and place: *Johnny Tremain* takes place in revolutionary Boston. The story could not take place anywhere else or at any other time. Ray Bradbury's *The Most Dangerous Game* requires an isolated, uninhabited island for its plot.

Settings are sometimes changed in a work to represent different periods of a person's life or to compare and contrast life in the city or life in the country.

Point of View:

The point of view is the perspective of the person who is the focus of the work of fiction: a story told in the first person is from the point of view of the narrator. In more modern works, works told in the third person usually concentrate on the point of view of one character or else the changes in point of view are clearly delineated, as in *Cold Mountain* by Charles Frazier, who names each chapter after the person whose point of view is being shown. Sudden, unexplained shifts in point of view—i.e., going into the thoughts of one character after another within a short space of time—are a sign of amateurish writing.

SKILL I.A.4 **Knows the defining characteristics of major forms within each primary literary genre (e.g., poetry: ballad, haiku).**
a. identify characteristics of major forms within each genre through distinctions in structure and content (e.g., sonnets versus ballads, satire versus realism)

Poetic Terminology

• *Rhyme*: Indicates a repeated end sound of lines or words within a poem. Rhymes usually occur at the ends of lines, though they can also be internal.

Example:

"Because I could not stop for Death
He kindly stopped for me
The Carriage held but just Ourselves
And Immortality."

         – Emily Dickinson, "Because I could not stop for Death."

"Me" and "Immortality" rhyme in this poem, lending a sense of finality to the last line and giving it a pleasing rhythm.

• *Rhyme scheme*: The pattern of rhymes in each line of a poem. Rhyme schemes are usually indicated with letters. Some poets follow strict rhyme schemes, some shirk them entirely, but most employ repetitive rhyme schemes when aesthetically appropriate and then subvert them for stronger effect.

Example:

"A wonderful bird is the pelican;
His beak can hold more than his belly-can.
He can hold in his beak
Enough food for a week,
Though I'm damned if I know how the hell-he-can!"

         — Dixon Lanier Merritt

This is an example of a limerick—a short, humorous poem employing a five line rhyme scheme. Limericks always follow an AABBA rhyme scheme. The first two lines rhyme, the next two shorter lines have a different rhyme, and the fifth line calls back to the original rhyme. Limerick structure is intentionally simplistic, highlighting the absurdity of the subject matter and allowing the poet to focus more on wordplay. The B rhymes of the third and fourth lines build anticipation for the final reveal on the fifth line, where the author can reveal a witty subversion.

• *Slant Rhyme*: A slant rhyme is also known as a "near rhyme," "half rhyme" or "lazy rhyme." Slant rhymes sometimes have the same vowel sounds but different consonants, or the reverse. Slant rhymes are sometimes considered childish or uncreative, but many poets of have made use of them in order to avoid clichés, to create disharmony in a piece, or to draw unusual connections between words.

Example:

"When have I last looked on
The round green eyes and the long wavering bodies
Of the dark leopards of the moon?
All the wild witches, those most noble ladies"

         — W. B. Yeats, "Lines Written in Dejection"

"On" and "moon" are slant rhymes, as are "bodies" and "ladies." This could be said to suggest the author's discordant, dejected state of mind. Perhaps in a happier poem these rhymes would be clearer and more musical. But not here.

• *Stanza*: A group of lines, offset by punctuation or spacing, forming a metrical unit or verse in a poem.

Example:
"Do not go gentle into that good night,
Old age should burn and rave at close of day;
Rage, rage against the dying of the light.

Though wise men at their end know dark is right,
Because their words had forked no lightning they
Do not go gentle into that good night."
— Dylan Thomas, "Do not go gentle into that good night."

Each short stanza contains three lines and ends with either "do not go gentle into that good night" or "rage, rage against the dying of the light." This end rhyme repeats throughout the entire poem, ensuring that each stanza delivers the essential message in a profound and affecting way.

• *Meter*: The basic rhythmic structure of a poem, the "music" of it. Some poetic forms prescribe their own metrical structure, but other poets invented or modified their own.

Example:
"Shall I compare thee to a summer's day?
Thou art more lovely and more temperate /
Rough winds do shake the darling buds of May,
And summer's lease hath all too short a date."
— William Shakespeare, "Sonnet 18."

Almost any poem could be said to have some form of meter, but Shakespeare's "iambic pentameter" is among the most famous styles. This metrical style is divided into "iambs," five of them per line, each containing a stressed and unstressed syllable. The pattern could be described as "ba-BUM, ba-BUM, ba-BUM," not unlike the beating of a heart. This metrical rhythm permeates Shakespeare's work, proving very attractive to actors who appreciate the clear, emphatic delivery.

• *Alliteration*: The use of repeated sounds at the start of words in quick succession. Alliteration is often used to draw attention to specific words or sounds, to lend emphasis to specific aspects of the poem. It can also be used to provide an entertaining and engaging voice to a poem.

Example:

"One short sleepe past, wee wake eternally,
And death shall be no more; death, thou shalt die."
                    — John Donne, "Death Be Not Proud."

In this poem, the alliterative W and D sounds draw parallels between their respective words, and create a vocal punctuation for the line. A D sound begins the last line and a D sound ends it, creating a sense of urgency, of continuity and finality in the line.

• *Assonance*: Similar to alliteration, except that the repeated sounds are contained within certain words.

Example:

"And miles to go before I sleep
And miles to go before I sleep."

The repeated O sounds create a sense of speed and urgency. The sound carries us through the line, creating contrast with the E sound in "sleep," where both the narrator and reader finally rest.

• *Enjambment*: An enjambed line flows into the next line without a break. No punctuation divides one line from the next. The line simply continues.

Example:

"April is the cruellest month, breeding
Lilacs out of the dead land, mixing
Memory and desire, stirring
Dull roots with spring rain."
                    — T. S. Eliot, "The Waste Land."

Eliot's use of enjambment in "The Waste Land" creates a sense of suspense in the poem. The action of breeding, mixing, and stirring are lent equal or superior importance to the actual subject, *April*. The enjambment also creates a slant rhyme as well, with each line ending on an "-ing" until we arrive at "rain."

• *Free Verse*: Poetry that avoids an identifiable meter or rhyme scheme could be said to be "free." The style became more popular amongst avant-garde, modern, and postmodern poets. It was comparatively rare in classical poetry.

Example:

i carry your heart with me (i carry it in
my heart) i am never without it (anywhere
i go you go, my dear; and whatever is done
by only me is your doing, my darling)
                    — e e cummings, "i carry your heart with me."

Cummings' style shirked literary conventions, creating poems that challenged traditional assumptions about form and aesthetic appeal through his use of strange capitalization, heavy enjambment, and free verse. Cummings' poems sometimes defy clear explanation, but some critics suggest he wrote in this manner to evoke a childish, earnest state of mind.

• *Metaphor*: An indirect comparison between two things, denoting one object or action in place of another to suggest a comparison between them. This is distinct from a simile, which directly compares two things using words such as "like" or "as."

Example:
"I'm a riddle in nine syllables,
An elephant, a ponderous house,
A melon strolling on two tendrils.
red fruit, ivory, fine timbers!"
— Sylvia Plath, "Metaphors."

Appropriately enough, Sylvia Plath's "Metaphors" contains several playful metaphors used to describe her pregnancy. Plath uses herself as a subject, comparing her pregnant state to an elephant, a melon, and in several ways to a shelter for the life growing inside her. At first the metaphors seem self-deprecating and humorous, but later in the poem, where she calls herself a "means, a stage" and mentions how she's "boarded the train there's no getting off," the metaphors take on darker connotation as they reflect her dehumanization and resigned acceptance that she's become merely an incubator for the child she now carries.

• *Sonnet*: A poetic form that originated in Italy, consisting of fourteen lines which follow a clear alternating rhyme scheme. Conventions of sonnets have shifted through the centuries, and the form has proved popular in England, Italy, and France.

Example:
Do not stand at my grave and weep:
I am not there; I do not sleep.
I am a thousand winds that blow,
I am the diamond glints on snow,
I am the sun on ripened grain,
I am the gentle autumn rain.
When you awaken in the morning's hush
I am the swift uplifting rush
Of quiet birds in circling flight.
I am the soft starshine at night.
Do not stand at my grave and cry:
I am not there; I did not die.
— Mary Elizabeth Frye, "Do not stand at my grave and weep."

This sonnet showcases much of what is attractive about the form to poets. The simple rhyme scheme is unpretentious and readable, and the poem's format lends itself well to repetition. The repeated "I am's" create a soothing rhythm, sort of a lullaby quality.

The subject matter is bittersweet, as with many sonnets that have explored romance, mortality, or spirituality. The first and last two lines mirror each other, suggesting change and finality. The poem's subject matter insists we not fear the end, and this is reflected in the sonnet's form.

• *Imagery*: Any sequence of words that refers to a sensory experience can be considered imagery. Rather than merely describing the visual aspect of something, imagery often relies on taste, touch, smell, or sound to draw a fuller portrait of the subject.

Example:

"Whirl up, sea—
Whirl your pointed pines,
Splash your great pines
On our rocks,
Hurl your green over us—
Cover us with your pools of fir."
          — Hilda Doolittle, "O read."

Doolittle's poem neatly encapsulates a style known as *Imagism*, a short-lived movement in the early 20th century that sought to reduce poetic language to its barest components. Each line, each word in this poem reveals something new. Doolittle likens a forest to a sea (or perhaps a sea to a forest), encouraging us to imagine green trees like torrential waves, evoking sound, color, and texture to maintain this dual metaphor. The poem is unique in that there is no "correct" image. Both the sea and the forest are equally valid interpretations of this poem, drawn together by their shared sensory features.

Onomatopoeia: A "sound effect," a word that imitates that actual sound it describes. "Buzz" or "hiss" both sound like the actions of buzzing or hissing.

Example:

"I chatter over stony ways,
In little sharps and trebles,
I bubble into eddying bays,
I babble on the pebbles."
          — Alfred, Lord Tennyson, "The Brook."

The onomatopoeia in Tennyson's "The Brook" evokes the sounds of its subject. The assonant B and T sounds suggest the burbling of a river, water running over rocks.

• *Personification*: When human qualities are applied to a non-human entity, such as an animal, an emotion, an object, or something more esoteric.

Example:

"Let the rain kiss you
Let the rain beat upon your head with silver liquid drops
Let the rain sing you a lullaby"
            — Langston Hughes, "April Rain Song."

In this poem, Hughes suggests that the rain has the human ability to kiss and to sing. Rather than merely describing pleasant, "realistic" aspects of rain, he personifies it as a friendly, motherly figure to better describe his feelings towards rain.

• *Couplet*: A pair of rhyming lines with the same meter. A "heroic couplet" is a couplet in iambic pentameter that is "self-contained" and not enjambed. Shakespeare often ended his sonnets with a heroic couplet, allowing the piece to build towards a climactic, self-contained final rhyme that delivered the sonnet's chief message.

Example:

"Sol thro' white Curtains shot a tim'rous Ray,
And op'd those Eyes that must eclipse the Day;
Now Lapdogs give themselves the rowzing Shake,
And sleepless Lovers, just at Twelve, awake:"
            — Alexander Pope, "Rape of the Lock."

Pope's "Rape of the Lock" is a satirical narrative poem written entirely in heroic couplets. The subject matter of the piece, regarding a baron's attempts to gain a lock of a woman's hair, is silly and banal. Thus, the constant use of triumphant, heroic couplets renders the whole thing a bizarre parody.

• *Narrative poem*: Appropriately enough, a narrative poem is a poem that tells a story. It can make use of narrators, characters, plot, setting, and other literary devices, though they often contain more poetic features, such as rhyme, meter, and metaphor. An "epic poem" is a type of narrative poem that's usually lengthy and recounts heroic deeds and mythology.

Example:

"By the shore of Gitche Gumee,
By the shining Big-Sea-Water,
At the doorway of his wigwam,
In the pleasant Summer morning,
Hiawatha stood and waited."
            — Henry Wadsworth Longfellow, "The Song of Hiawatha"

Longfellow's epic poem, "The Song of Hiawatha," recalls the mythologized exploits of the titular Native American hero. Hiawatha is based on a few historical persons, but as with much epic poetry, his exploits are expanded into something superhuman.

When setting out to interpret a poem, authorial intention is a good starting point. What message was the author intending to convey with the piece? Read it through a few times, and pause to consider words or references you don't understand. Start with the easy solution, not every poem is a labyrinth of mysterious interpretations. Consider the fact that, in an enduring poem, nothing happens by accident. Each line, each word was selected very carefully by the poet for a specific effect. This will allow you to go deeper off of your original assessment of the poem, and to infer the meaning of unclear references and unusual devices.

See also Skill I.A.3.

SKILL I.A.5 Understands how textual evidence supports interpretations of a literary text.
a. comprehend the literal and figurative meanings of a text
b. draw inferences from the text
c. determine the textual evidence that supports an analysis of the literary text

As a teacher, you will be required to instruct your students in literary interpretation. To do this, you'll need to understand the modes of literary interpretation, yourself. The key is specificity. Interpretation must be grounded in the factual, literal text of the story. Praxis test-givers want to see your understanding of the nuts-and-bolts of a work. Your impression can be as imaginative as you desire, but you'll need to cite sources and provide direct quotes.

First comes the easy part – the literal interpretation of the text. What happens? Who are the characters and what do they do? For non-fiction, what is the thesis? The message? Any work, no matter how abstract, can be pared down to a paragraph summary.

Here is an example. The following is one of the most revered poems in the English canon, "Ozymandias" by Percy Bysshe Shelley. Read it through, and see what your initial reactions are. Try reading it out loud as well. Some poems are better understood when heard.

> I met a traveller from an antique land
>
> Who said: "Two vast and trunkless legs of stone
>
> Stand in the desert . . . Near them, on the sand,
>
> Half sunk, a shattered visage lies, whose frown,
>
> And wrinkled lip, and sneer of cold command,
>
> Tell that its sculptor well those passions read

Which yet survive, stamped on these lifeless things,

The hand that mocked them, and the heart that fed:

And on the pedestal these words appear:

'My name is Ozymandias, king of kings:

Look on my works, ye Mighty, and despair!'

Nothing beside remains. Round the decay

Of that colossal wreck, boundless and bare

The lone and level sands stretch far away."

First, you might summarize the piece to demonstrate your comprehension. Our narrator is unnamed, and the story is second hand, a tale he recalls from some traveler from an "antique land". The traveler describes a two pillars of stone he found in the endless desert, and next to them lay a shattered stone face, well-carved but slowly eroding away. Beside the face is a pedestal telling of some "king of kings", Ozymandias, who declares his "works" would cause even the mighty to despair. What "works" this describes is not clear to the traveler, for they seem to have crumbled to dust in the endless centuries, leaving only sand as far as the eye can see.

This literal interpretation inevitably leads to the figurative one. Ask yourself, why is this important? Why did Shelley find this story necessary to recount?

To answer this, we need to look past what is literally stated to find out what is implied. We can infer that the pedestal once referred to some grander structure, a monument perhaps, or maybe a castle or city. The face and pillars, at the very least, likely towered above the desert, depicting their fearsome subject for all to see. Surely this Ozymandias must have been wealthy to erect such a large sculpture, and it is telling that he wished to be depicted with a commanding sneer. The face was carved by some sculptor who either feared or greatly revered his subject. Ozymandias fancied himself a conqueror, one who would inspire awe in all who see saw his monument.

But it did not last. The monument is crumbling, the desert around it is bare. Even this traveler from his "antique land" knows nothing of great Ozymandias except what he read on some plinth in the desert. Why did Ozymandias fade from memory? Who can say? Whatever great and terrible things Ozymandias accomplished, it was not enough to save him or his memory from the ravages of time.

The pedestal thus becomes sadly ironic – whereas once the mighty may have despaired upon seeing a fearsome monument that dwarfed them, today they will despair upon seeing that even the "king of kings", Ozymandias, has been forgotten for all time, his great accomplishments lost to the ages. One could interpret this as a musing on mortality, or perhaps as a more political screed about the fleeting nature of power and wealth. Shelley is trying to teach us that even the mightiest of conquerors can die and be forgotten. Time waits for no man.

Whatever interpretation you pursue, you must anchor it to the piece with direct references to the text. For instance, the poem is a sonnet, though not a typical one. There is a rhyme scheme but it is far less pronounced than in most sonnets – it makes frequent use of slant rhymes, such as "stone" and "frown" or "fear" and "despair", and the enjambment of the piece alters its flow, preventing "sing-song" rhymes from appearing. It also contains no heroic couplet, the poem also features iambic pentameter, though it is less pronounced than in works such as Shakespeare's. Each line contains five iambs of two syllables each, with exactly one exception: line 10, "my name is Ozymandias", breaks the ten-syllable pattern, offering eleven syllables instead.

Perhaps these were poetic choices by Shelley to render the poem noble yet solemn. He evokes the vaunted poetic style of Shakespeare, but dirties it up, so to speak. The very structure of the piece is a "broken" tribute to the past, like the plinth in the desert. Likewise, Ozymandias's eleven-syllable introductory line sets him apart from the rest of the poem, and gives him greater import. These clear structural deviations are all worth mentioning in your interpretation of this piece. Anytime an author breaks an established pattern, they want you to notice.

SKILL I.A.6 **Understands how authors develop themes in a variety of genres.**
a. identify the themes and/or central ideas of a given text
b. analyze how a theme or central idea is developed throughout one or more texts
c. recognize universal themes from myths, traditional stories, or religious works and how they are rendered or alluded to in literary works

---

"Theme" refers to the central topic, idea, or statement of a literary work. Some themes are opaque, such as in fables, cautionary tales, or morality plays which exist primarily to educate or warn their audience, or impart a cultural value. Some themes are subtler and require close reading to discern. All literature can be said to possess some sort of theme, and it is up to the teacher to discern these themes and present them to the class in such a way that the students can clearly see the connection.

To identify the theme of the work, ask yourself, what is the moral? What does the author want you to think about the subject? What statements or commentary is the author trying to make?

This analysis also requires familiarity with tone, the mood or emotional underpinning of the piece. Franz Kafka's works deal frequently with the theme of bureaucracy, and one can clearly tell his attitude is sharply critical of these institutions due to his dark, foreboding tales about harried protagonists being destroyed by the system for reasons unclear. George Orwell's works are even more opaque. *Animal Farm* is an allegory about the rise of totalitarianism in Russia, and a close reading of the text reveals numerous historical references that reveal the work as sharply critical.

Some themes might not be central to the work, but can still create deeper engagement with the piece. The primary themes of the *Harry Potter* series, for instance, are love, bravery, and growing up, but the series frequently makes use of subplots that reveal sharp commentary on more specific topics: the media, racism, and abusive relationships, to name a few.

Some themes are universal, stretching back millennia to the earliest campfire tales. These first oral tellings sought to explain the various natural phenomena early humans encountered, and to impart cultural beliefs to the next generation. Death is a common theme in all mythology. Many cultures personify death to better explain it, creating various gods or mythological figures to embody the concept, such as the Greeks' Hades, Anubis of Egyptian myth, or the variety of artworks belonging to the "Danse Macabre" genre of Middle Ages European art, which depicted the dead as spritely figures dancing amongst the living.

Social hierarchy is another common theme, one that has shifted drastically throughout history. Early tales usually espoused the value of social order, depicting a king who is anointed by the gods to rule, and having the story end when order is restored and the royalty succeeds. In the past centuries, works have shifted to be more critical of traditional social roles. 20th century political satire criticizes the hierarchy we find ourselves subject to.

SKILL I.A.7 **Understands how literary elements (e.g. characterization, setting, tone) contribute to the meaning of a text.**
  a. analyze the impact of differences in the points of view of characters and/or narrators
  b. analyze the structure of a plot
  c. analyze how different elements contribute to mood, tone, and conflict
  d. analyze how particular lines of dialogue or story events impact meaning
  e. analyze the text for character development

The analysis of a piece of literature calls for attention to structural elements so as to discern meaning, purpose, and themes. The author's intentions are gleaned through the elements he or she uses and how they are used. It's critical for the teacher to deeply analyze all structural elements (plot, characters, setting, and point of view). This will assist your students in their own analytical endeavors.

The "plot" of a story is the sequence of events (it may or may not be chronological) that the author chooses to represent the story to be told--both the underlying story and the externals of the occurrences the author relates. An author may use "flashbacks" to tell the back story (or what went before the current events begin). Often, authors begin their stories in media res, or in the middle of things, and, over time, supply the details of what has gone before to provide a clearer picture to the reader of all the relevant events.

Sometimes authors tell parallel stories in order to make their points. For example, in Count Leo Tolstoy's classic Anna Karenina, the unhappy extramarital affair of Anna Karenina and Count Vronsky is contrasted with the happy marriage of Lev and Kitty through the use of alternating chapters devoted to each couple. The plot consists of the progress of each couple: Anna and Count Vronsky into deeper neurosis, obsession, and emotional pain, and Lev and Kitty into deeper and more meaningful partnership through growing emotional intimacy, parenthood, and caring for members of their extended family.

In good novels, each part of the plot is necessary and has a purpose. For example, in Anna Karenina, a chapter is devoted to a horse race Count Vronsky participates in. This might seem like mere entertainment, but, in fact, Count Vronsky is riding his favorite mare, and, in a moment of carelessness in taking a jump, puts the whole weight of his body on the mare's back, breaking it. The horse must be shot. Vronsky loved and admired the mare, but being overcome by a desire to win, he kills the very thing he loves. Similarly, Anna descends into obsession and jealousy as their affair isolates her from society and separates her from her child, and ultimately kills herself. The chapter symbolizes the destructive effect Vronsky's love, coupled with inordinate desire, has upon what and whom he loves.

Other authors use repetitious plot lines to reveal the larger story over time. For example, in Joseph Heller's satirical novel Catch-22, the story continually returns to a horrific incident in an airplane while flying a combat mission. Each time the protagonist, Yossarian, recalls the incident, more detail is revealed. The reader knows from the beginning that this incident is key to why Yossarian wants to be discharged from the army, but it is not until the full details of the gruesome incidents are revealed late in the book that the reader knows why the incident has driven Yossarian almost mad. Interspersed with comedic and ironic episodes, the book's climax (the full revealing of the incident) remains powerfully with the reader, showing the absurdity, insanity, and inhumanity of war. The comic device of Catch-22, a fictitious army rule from which the title is derived, makes this point in a funny way: Catch-22 states that a soldier cannot be discharged from the army unless he is crazy; yet, if he wants to be discharged from the army, he is not crazy. This rule seems to embody the insanity, absurdity, and inhumanity of war.

Characters usually represent or embody an idea or ideal acting in the world. For example, in the Harry Potter series, Harry Potter's goodness, courage and unselfishness, as well as his capacity for friendship and love, make him a powerful opponent to Voldemort, whose selfishness, cruelty, and isolation make him the leader of the evil forces in the epic battle of good versus evil. Memorable characters are many-sided: Harry is not only brave, strong, and true, he is vulnerable and sympathetic: orphaned as a child, bespectacled, and often misunderstood by his peers, Harry is not a stereotypical hero.

Charles Dickens's Oliver Twist is the principle of goodness, oppressed and unrecognized, unleashed in a troubled world. Oliver encounters a great deal of evil, which he refuses to cooperate with, and also a great deal of good in people who have sympathy for his plight. In contrast to the gentle, kindly, and selfless Maylies who take Oliver in, recognizing his goodness, are the evil Bill Sykes and Fagin—thieves and murderers—who are willing to sell and hurt others for their own gain. When Nancy, a thief in league with Sykes and Fagin, essentially "sells" herself to help Oliver, she represents redemption from evil through sacrifice.

The setting of a work of fiction adds a great deal to the story. Historical fiction relies firmly on an established time and place: *Johnny Tremain* takes place in revolutionary Boston; the story could not take place anywhere else or at any other time. Ray Bradbury's *The Most Dangerous Game* requires an isolated, uninhabited island for its plot. Settings are sometimes changed in a work to represent different periods of a person's life or to compare and contrast life in the city or life in the country.

The point of view is the perspective of the person who is the focus of the work of fiction: a story told in the first person is from the point of view of the narrator. In more modern works, works told in the third person usually concentrate on the point of view of one character or else the changes in point of view are clearly delineated, as in *Cold Mountain* by Charles Frazier, who names each chapter after the person whose point of view is being shown. Sudden, unexplained shifts in point of view—i.e., going into the thoughts of one character after another within a short space of time—are a sign of amateurish writing.

SKILL I.A.8 **Understands how figurative language contributes to the effect of a text.**
a. identify examples of various types of figurative language (e.g., extended metaphor, imagery, hyperbole)
b. interpret figurative language in context and analyze its role in the text

Figurative Devices

Figurative language allows for the statement of truths that more literal language cannot. Figures of speech add many dimensions of richness to our writing and allow many opportunities for worthwhile analysis. Skillfully used, a figure of speech will help the reader, see more clearly and focus upon particulars. Listing all possible figures of speech is beyond the scope of this list. However, for purposes of building vocabulary, a few are sufficient.

Parallelism: The arrangement of ideas in phrases, sentences, and paragraphs that balance one element with another of equal importance and similar wording. Here is an example from Francis Bacon's *Of Studies:*

"Reading maketh a full man, conference a ready man, and writing an exact man."

Euphemism: The substitution of an agreeable or inoffensive term for one that might offend or suggest something unpleasant. Many euphemisms are used to refer to death to avoid using the word, such as "passed away," "crossed over," or "passed."

Hyperbole: Deliberate exaggeration for dramatic or comic effect. Here is an example from Shakespeare's The Merchant of Venice:

> "Why, if two gods should play some heavenly match
> And on the wager lay two earthly women,
> And Portia one, there must be something else
> Pawned with the other, for the poor rude world
> Hath not her fellow."

Bathos: A ludicrous attempt to portray pathos—that is, to evoke pity, sympathy, or sorrow. It may result from inappropriately dignifying the commonplace, using elevated language to describe something trivial, or greatly exaggerating pathos.

Oxymoron: A contradiction in terms deliberately employed for effect. It is usually seen in a qualifying adjective whose meaning is contrary to that of the noun it modifies, such as "wise folly."

Irony: Expressing something other than and often opposite of the literal meaning, such as words of praise when blame is intended. In poetry, it is often used as a sophisticated or resigned awareness of contrast between what is and what ought to be and expresses a controlled pathos without sentimentality. It is a form of indirection that avoids overt praise or censure. An early example is the Greek comic character Eiron, a clever underdog who by his wit repeatedly triumphs over the boastful character Alazon.

Malapropism: A verbal blunder in which one word is replaced by another similar in sound but different in meaning. This term comes from Sheridan's Mrs. Malaprop in

The Rivals (1775). Thinking of the geography of contiguous countries, she spoke of the "geometry" of "contagious countries."

Other common figurative devices include: simile, metaphor, alliteration, onomatopoeia, personification. These are included in the chapter on poetry for AP English Language and Composition included with this study guide.

Other Syntax Devices

Synonyms and antonyms: A synonym means the same thing as another word and can substitute for it in certain contexts. Diversifying vocabulary in your writing by incorporating synonyms will improve your writing, giving you the best chance for a high score on the written sections for AP exams.

Original word	Synonyms
Smart	Intelligent, bright
Required	Necessary, mandatory
Many	Numerous

An antonym represents a meaning opposite that of a given word.

Original word	Antonym
Optional	Required
Before	After
Complex	Simple

Analogies: An analogy illustrates an idea by means of a more familiar idea that is similar or parallel to it. These are commonly found on AP exams, and studying vocabulary and literary devices will help you in breaking down meaning to find the correct answers. As you read through options for analogies in the multiple choice sections, it's important to keep in mind that you're looking for the most logical answer. Beware of questions that have multiple options that make sense, and try to zero in on the "best" answer. Also, it's best to go with your gut answer while determining the correct option for analogies. Over thinking will lead to second guessing. You could waste valuable test time as you continue to run through the possibilities.

Most commonly, analogies are laid out on AP exams like this:

An apple is to fruit as _____ is to vegetable.

    A. Celery
    B. Water
    C. Organic
    D. Hydroponic

The clear answer for the above question is A. Celery. You may find analogies on AP exams that stem from cause/effect, part of a whole, and characteristics (similar or complete opposite).

Idioms: An idiom is a word or expression that cannot be translated word for word into another language, such as "I am running low on gas." By extension, writers use idioms to convey a way of speaking and writing typical of a group of people. Some idioms are passed down from one generation to the next, but not all. Because language is constantly evolving, some idioms are left behind while new phrases come into use. For example, the saying "burn the midnight oil," meaning working late into the night, has died off. This may have been a common saying around the time oil lamps were used, but technology has evolved to the point this saying would be arbitrary to our current society. Listed below are some common idioms in American English:

- Birthday suit
- Down the drain
- Show off
- At the drop of a hat
- Taste of your own medicine
- Piece of cake
- Keep an eye on it
- Long shot
- Play it by ear
- Raining cats and dogs
- An arm and a leg
- Sick as a dog

Dialect: Dialect, also referred to as regionalism, includes usages that are peculiar to a particular part of a country. A good example is the second-person plural pronoun you. Because the plural is the same as the singular, speakers in various parts of the country have developed their own vocabulary solutions to be sure that they are understood when they are speaking to more than one "you." In the South, "you-all" or "y'all" is common. In the Northeast, one often hears "youse." In some areas of the Midwest, "you'ns" can be heard. Similar to idiomatic expressions, dialect evolves to incorporate societal trends and expands from year to year.

Jargon: Jargon is a specialized vocabulary. It may be the vocabulary peculiar to a particular industry, such as computers, or of a field of interest, such as religion. It may also be the vocabulary of a social group. The jargon of bloggers comprises a whole vocabulary that has even developed its own dictionaries. The speaker must be knowledgeable about and sensitive to the jargon peculiar to the particular audience. That may require some research and some vocabulary development on the speaker's part. For example, technical language is a form of jargon. It is usually specific to an industry, profession, or field of study. Sensitivity to the language familiar to the particular audience is important.

> **SKILL I.A.9** **Understands how poetic devices and structure contribute to the effect of a poem.**
> a. analyze how poetic devices (e.g., rhyme scheme, rhythm, figurative language) contribute to meaning in a poem
> b. analyze how structure (e.g., stanza, free verse, concrete poem) contributes to meaning in a poem

See Skill I.A.3 and I.A.4.

> **SKILL I.A.10** **Understands how reading strategies (e.g. making predictions, making connections, summarizing) support comprehension.**
> a. identify literacy skills to support active reading (e.g. text-to-self connection, prediction, summarizing)
> b. evaluate a summary of a passage
> c. evaluate the strength of a prediction based on textual evidence

Critical reading involves dissecting the text to see the structure of the information presented and classify how things are said. This can be done to validate or repudiate what the author says. Students will become more engaged with a work if they can develop their own opinions and connections to it, so encourage them to connect the text to experiences in their own lives, to predict the outcome of the story, and to summarize what they've already read.

To determine the strength of a summary, you must identify the essential points of a passage and see if the student has caught them. What absolutely needed to happen in this section to make the story go forward? What needs to be described so that the rest of the story makes sense?

Some essential points in Act 1 of *Romeo & Juliet* are: Romeo is heartbroken over his breakup with Rosaline, there is strife between the Capulets and Montagues, and Romeo meets Juliet and falls madly in love. These points contextualize the rest of the play, and set the foundation for the famously tragic climax.

Likewise, students can form predictions based on these plot points. If there is conflict between the two families, students can safely predict this will come to a head in some way. There will likely be violence, as the play opens with entourages from both houses openly threatening each other. Students can also infer that Romeo and Juliet's relationship will develop. Perhaps they might predict there will be a happy ending, that the two lovers' relationship will mend the rift between their houses. Even though this prediction is wrong, it can still deepen the connection to the material, as they now have a vested interest in seeing the tragedy play out.

Children's books are a reflection of both developmental theories and social changes. Reading provides children with the opportunity to become more aware of societal differences, to measure their behavior against the behavior of realistic fictional characters or the subjects of biographies, to become informed about events of the past and present that will affect their futures, and to acquire a genuine appreciation of literature.

> **SKILL I.A.11** **Knows commonly used research-based strategies for reading instruction (e.g., activating prior knowledge, modeling metacognitive practices, active reading).**
> a. recognize commonly used research-based strategies for teaching reading (e.g., activating prior knowledge, modeling metacognitive practices)
> b. evaluate the effectiveness of specific strategies to support a particular reading task
> c. interpret research and apply it to particular reading instruction challenges

As educators, we have an obligation to guide children in the selection of books that are appropriate to their reading ability and interest levels. Of course, there is a fine line between guidance and censorship. As with discipline, parents learn that to make forbidden is to make more desirable. To publish a list of banned books is to make them suddenly attractive. Most children/adolescents left to their own selections will choose books on topics that interest them and are written in language they can understand.

Social changes since World War II have significantly affected adolescent literature. The civil rights movements, feminism, the protest of the Vietnam War, and issues surrounding homelessness, neglect, teen pregnancy, drugs, and violence all have given rise to contemporary fiction that helps adolescents understand and cope with the world they live in.

Popular books for preadolescents deal more with establishing relationships with members of the opposite sex and learning to cope with their changing bodies, personalities, or life situations, as in Judy Blume's Are You There, God? It's Me,

Margaret. Adolescents find interest in the fantasy and science fiction genres as well as popular juvenile fiction. Middle school students might enjoy reading the Little House on the Prairie series and the mysteries of the Hardy Boys and Nancy Drew. Teens value the works of Emily and Charlotte Brontë, Willa Cather, Jack London, William Shakespeare, Mark Twain, and J. R. R. Tolkien as much as those of Piers Anthony, S. E. Hinton, Suzanne Collins, Madeleine L'Engle, Stephen King, J. K. Rowling, and Stephenie Meyer because they're fun to read whatever their underlying literary worth may be.

Older adolescents enjoy the writers in these genres:
- Fantasy: Piers Anthony, Ursula K. LeGuin, Anne McCaffrey
- Horror: V. C. Andrews, Stephen King
- Juvenile fiction: Judy Blume, Robert Cormier, Rosa Guy, Virginia Hamilton, S. E. Hinton, M. E. Kerr, Harry Mazer, Norma Fox Mazer, Richard Newton Peck, Cynthia Voigt, Paul Zindel
- Science fiction: Isaac Asimov, Ray Bradbury, Arthur C. Clarke, Frank Herbert, Larry Niven, H. G. Wells

These classic and contemporary works combine the characteristics of multiple theories. Functioning at the concrete operations stage (Piaget), being of the "good person" orientation (Kohlberg), still highly dependent on external rewards (Bandura), and exhibiting all five needs previously discussed from Maslow's hierarchy, eleven to twelve-year-olds should appreciate the following titles, grouped by reading level. These titles are also cited for interest at that grade level and do not reflect high-interest titles for older readers who do not read at grade level.

Reading level 6.0 to 6.9

Barrett, William. *Lilies of the Field*
Cormier, Robert. *Other Bells for Us to Ring*
Dahl, Roald. *Danny, Champion of the World; Charlie and the Chocolate Factory*
Lindgren, Astrid. *Pippi Longstocking*
Lindbergh, Anne. *Three Lives to Live*
Lowry, Lois. *Rabble Starkey*
Naylor, Phyllis. *The Year of the Gopher; Reluctantly Alice*
Peck, Robert Newton. *Arly*
Speare, Elizabeth. *The Witch of Blackbird Pond*
Sleator, William. *The Boy Who Reversed Himself*

For seventh and eighth grades

Most seventh- and eighth-grade students, according to learning theory, are still functioning cognitively, psychologically, and morally as sixth graders. As these are not inflexible standards, there are some twelve- and thirteen-year-olds who are much more mature socially, intellectually, and physically than the younger children who share the same school. They are becoming concerned with establishing individual and peer group identities, and this can present conflicts with established authority and rigid rules. Some at this age are still tied firmly to the family and its expectations, while others identify more with those their own age or older.

Enrichment reading for this group must help them cope with life's rapid changes or provide escape and thus must be either realistic or fantastic depending on the child's needs. Adventures and mysteries (the Hardy Boys and Nancy Drew series) are still popular today. Preteens also become more interested in biographies of contemporary figures than those of legendary figures of the past.

Reading level 7.0 to 7.9

Armstrong, William. *Sounder*
Bagnold, Enid. *National Velvet*
Barrie, James. *Peter Pan*
London, Jack. *White Fang; Call of the Wild*
Lowry, Lois. *Taking Care of Terrific*
McCaffrey, Anne. *The Dragonsinger series*
Montgomery, L. M. *Anne of Green Gables and sequels*
Steinbeck, John. *The Pearl*
Tolkien, J. R. R. *The Hobbit*
Zindel, Paul. *The Pigman*

Reading level 8.0 to 8.9

Cormier, Robert. *I Am the Cheese*
McCullers, Carson. *The Member of the Wedding*
North, Sterling. *Rascal*
Twain, Mark. *The Adventures of Tom Sawyer*
Zindel, Paul. *My Darling, My Hamburger*

For ninth grade

Depending upon the school environment, a ninth grader may be top dog in a junior high school or underdog in a high school. Much of ninth graders' social development and thus their reading interests become motivated by their peer associations. Ninth graders are technically adolescents operating at the early stages of formal operations in cognitive development. Their perception of their own identity is becoming well defined, and they are fully aware of the ethics required by society. These students are more receptive to the challenges of classic literature but still enjoy popular teen novels.

Reading level 9.0 to 9.9

Brown, Dee. *Bury My Heart at Wounded Knee*
Defoe, Daniel. *Robinson Crusoe*
Dickens, Charles. *David Copperfield*
Greenberg, Joanne. *I Never Promised You a Rose Garden*
Kipling, Rudyard. *Captains Courageous*
Mathabane, Mark. *Kaffir Boy*
Nordhoff, Charles. *Mutiny on the Bounty*
Shelley, Mary. *Frankenstein*
Washington, Booker T. *Up From Slavery*

For tenth through twelfth grades

All high school sophomores, juniors, and seniors can handle most other literature except for a few of the most difficult titles like Moby–Dick or Vanity Fair. However, since many high school students do not progress to the eleventh- or twelfth-grade reading level, they will still have their favorites among authors whose writings they can understand.

Many will struggle with assigned novels but still read high-interest books for pleasure. A few high-interest titles are listed below without reading level designations, though most are 6.0 to 7.9.

Bauer, Joan. *Squashed*
Borland, Hal. *When the Legends Die*
Danzinger, Paula. *Remember Me to Herald Square*
Duncan, Lois. *Stranger with My Face*
Hamilton, Virginia. *The Planet of Junior Brown*
Hinton, S. E. *The Outsiders*
Paterson, Katherine. *The Great Gilly Hopkins*

Teachers of students at all levels must be familiar with the materials offered by the libraries in their own schools. Only then can they guide their students into appropriate selections for their social age and reading level development.

Adolescent literature, because of the age range of readers, is extremely diverse. Fiction for the middle group, usually ages 10–11 to 14–15, deals with issues of coping with internal and external changes in their lives. Because children's writers in the twentieth and twenty-first centuries have produced increasingly realistic fiction, adolescents can now find problems dealt with honestly in novels and short stories.

Teachers of middle/junior high school students see the greatest change in interests and reading abilities. Fifth- and sixth-graders, included in elementary grades in many schools, are viewed as older children, while seventh and eighth graders are seen as preadolescents. Ninth-graders, who are sometimes the highest class in junior high school and sometimes the lowest class in high school, definitely view themselves as teenagers. Their literature choices will often be governed more by interest than by ability; thus the wealth of high-interest, low-readability books that has flooded the market in recent years. Tenth- through twelfth-graders will still select high-interest books for pleasure reading but are also easily encouraged to stretch their abilities by reading more classics.

Because of rapid social changes, topics that once did not interest young people until they reached their teens—such as suicide, gangs, and homosexuality—are now subjects of books for younger readers. The plethora of high-interest books reveals how desperately schools have failed to produce on-level readers and how the market has adapted to that need. However, these high-interest books are now readable for younger children whose reading levels are at or above normal. No matter how tastefully written, some content is inappropriate for younger readers. The problem becomes not so much steering them toward books that they have the reading ability to handle but encouraging them toward books whose content is appropriate to their levels of cognitive and social development. A fifth-grader may be able to read V. C. Andrews' book Flowers in the Attic but not possess the social/moral development to handle the deviant behavior of the characters.

At the same time, because of the complex changes affecting adolescents, the teacher must be well versed in learning theory and child development and competent to teach the subject matter of language and literature.

> **SKILL**
> **I.A.12**
> **Is familiar with various literary theories (e.g., reader-response, feminist criticism) for interpreting and critiquing literary texts.**
> a. recognize ways literary theories are used to interpret and critique texts

Literary theory gives readers the opportunity to analyze texts from a variety of angles. These angles, also known as lenses, invite the reader, your student, to question different elements of a story to gain a better understanding of the true meaning behind the text. Biographical, sociological, economical, and stylistic influences can produce different meanings for the same text. One might consider the author's background, the time period in which they were raised, their religious outlook, their sexual orientation, their financial situation or social class, and their political views to further explore a work of writing. Intentional stylistic patterns, well-crafted literary devices, and a persuasive point of view also have an impact on the differences in meaning and interpretation.

Here is a list of the chief literary theories you should familiarize yourself with for testing purposes:
- Moral Criticism, Dramatic Construction – 360 BC
- New Criticism, Formalism – 1920s
- Structuralism – 1930s
- Psychoanalytic Criticism – 1930s
- Marxist Criticism – 1930s
- Reader-Response Criticism – 1960s
- Deconstruction – 1960s
- Feminist Criticism – 1960s

Moral Criticism, Dramatic Construction

The oldest form of literary theory, moral criticism examines literature based on its moral and ethical teachings. The earliest stories were oral tellings, parables designed to transfer cultural values from one generation to the next. Moral criticism focuses on this messaging, weighing a writing's merit by its relationship to the dominant morality of the time. Plato offered one of the earliest literary critiques in *Republic*, issuing his idea that art was an imperfect reproduction of nature, and as such was inherently corrupting unless it imparted strong moral values to its audience.

This attitude remained the dominant mode through which literature was discussed for millennia since. The various folk tales, fables, allegories, and "morality plays" of history sought to educate the youth about the dangers of greed, weakness, impiety, or whatever else the culture deems a moral failing at that time. Even today, the morality of a work is of great concern in certain genres – children's and young adult literature, for instance, if often critiqued along the lines of what is deemed appropriate or valuable for young people to hear.

Since cultural morals shift drastically over time and geography, moral criticism relies heavily on the perspective of the critic. The morality of a work's characters, author, or plot will always affect the opinion of a work from any critic, but moral criticism specifically measures the morality of a work as its barometer of merit. The more moral a work is, the better it is. Everything else is secondary.

New Criticism

New Criticism emphasizes the importance of both structure and semantics when doing an analysis of a text. External factors, such as the identity of the author, the society in which he or she lives, and the author's overall intentions for the work are not taken into consideration. Proponents of New Criticism believe that the literary text itself is the paramount concern.

When an analysis is performed, a text is evaluated and interpreted through what is called a "close reading." The goal of close reading is to arrive, without biographical or sociological distractions, at an objective understanding and appreciation of a literary work. Close reading emphasizes the relationship between the form in which the text is written and the meaning. Patterns within the text, imagery, point of view, and literary devices all play a role in determining the impact that form may have on overall meaning. The goal of close reading is to arrive, without biographical or sociological distractions, at an objective understanding and appreciation of a literary work.

The New Criticism's approach is summed up in two key literary anthologies: *Understanding Poetry* (4th ed.) and *Understanding Fiction*, both edited by Cleanth Brooks and Robert Penn Warren. Either one of these would be suitable as assigned texts for high school literature courses.

Structuralism and Deconstructionism

Like New Criticism, the structural approach does not take external influences into consideration to quantify certain criteria that a work must follow. Following the same guidelines of Formalism, emphasis is placed on the work itself, and its place within its literary style.

In deconstruction theory, only the text itself is examined. This is done through a very close reading. Formulated by Jacques Derrida in the 1960s, it has been unjustly called deconstructionism, as it takes an extremely detailed analytical approach. The text is broken down (deconstructed) and questioned piece by piece. A reader becomes more critical and skeptical when analyzing the intended meaning within the writing. The author's background and the context in which the text was written has no impact on the meaning.

Psychoanalytic, or Freudian, criticism

Based initially on the works of Sigmund Freud in the late 1800s, this theory has been expanded to include the ideas of other psychoanalysts. Freudian psychoanalysis holds that the human mind is a tripartite structure (divided into three parts) composed of:

- the id, which generates and seeks to satisfy all of a person's urges and desires;
- the superego, or empathy center, which "polices" and counters the id;
- and the ego, which is the psychic result of the id/superego conflict. The ego is characterized by a person's thoughts and behaviors.

All humans are said to have inexorable conflicts between drives such as Eros (the sex drive) and Thanatos (the death wish), which are also played out in the contests between id and superego. Neurotic behavior results from fixations on one of the above physical factors, or from an imbalance in the powers of the id and superego. Neurosis is usually rooted in infancy or early childhood.

The psychoanalytic literary critic applies Freudian theories to writings and authors in order to better understand the psychological underpinnings of literary works, writers, and, sometimes, society itself. Topics that will assist in analyzing a text from a Freudian perspective might include:

- The author's mental state

- Strange patterns of obsession or fascination (for example, death)

- The author's intention for provoking certain feelings in the reader

- Hidden meanings

- Evidence of writing in the subconscious

Writers that have garnered much attention from Freudian critics include Edgar Allen Poe, the Marquis de Sade, Moses, Madame de Stahl, and William S. Burroughs. Not surprisingly, sex and violence feature prominently in these writers' works. Representative examples of psychoanalytic criticism include "Moses and Monotheism" by Sigmund Freud, and *Edgar Allen Poe* by Marie Bonaparte.

Marxist Criticism

Based on the ideas of Karl Marx, Marxism takes the opposite approach when compared to New Criticism, Deconstructionism, and Structuralism. This lens focuses specifically on dialectic, environmental, and socioeconomic influence. For example, politics (particularly the capitalist system) and religion are easily identifiable when views are reflected within literature.

Some of the key components of this critical theory include:

- Conflicts within class systems that drive the history of human civilization.

- The capitalist or bourgeoisie (those who possess and control economic capital) exploitation and oppression of the proletariat (the working classes) for their own economic and political gains.

- The workers must therefore unite to overthrow the capitalists and their socio-economic system, resulting in a "dictatorship of the proletariat."

- Creating that will create a classless society in which most, if not all, private property is abolished in favor of collective ownership.

- Eventually the nation-states themselves will dissolve and be replaced by a unitary, worldwide communist-socialist society free of class conflict.

The Marxist orthodoxy holds that the triumph of communism is an inevitable triumph of capitalism, and that Marxist doctrine is validated by its scientific and materialist approach to history. Therefore, the Marxist critic uses these ideas to scrutinize literary works, which are analyzed and interpreted to determine their "revolutionary" or "proletarian," "bourgeois" or "reactionary," character. Works focused primarily on social injustice and abuses the abuse of power.

Feminist Criticism

Feminist critics emphasize the ways that literary works are informed and inspired by an author's gender, by their opinions about gender and gender roles, and by societal norms regarding gender in which the author has been immersed. Of prime concern to the feminist critical enterprise is the advocacy of women as intellectual, social, and artistic equals to men. Some feminists emphasize class, others race, and others sexual orientation when critiquing texts or social norms and conditions affecting women's lives. Feminist criticism is not limited to works by women, nor is it hostile to male writers or males in general. Many great feminist works have been written by men.

Women's rights advocacy is as old as history, but our modern interpretation of feminism began in the late 1800s with the rise of suffragism. This push for education and voting rights for women had a massive impact on media, allowing for inquiries into the role women play in our collective cultural voice. The "second wave" feminists of the 1960s, such as Gloria Steinem and Andrea Dworkin, further argued for the social and intellectual equality of women, and "third wave" feminists have broadened the literary conversation further to include topics relating to sexuality, orientation, and race.

Reader-Response

In this critical theory, the readers create meaning through their individual understandings and responses to a work. Some critics focus solely on the readers' experiences. Others experiment with defined groups to determine reader response. The author, context, and style of the text are all second to the reader's personal connection to the writing.

A pioneer in reader response theory, Louise Rosenblatt paved the way on the concept of treating the relationship between the reader and the text as a transaction. Her famous text, *Literature as Exploration*, explains and facilitates the interaction one might have with a piece of writing.

Informational Texts and Rhetoric

SKILL I.B.1 **Understands how textual evidence supports interpretations of an informational text.**
a. comprehend literal and figurative meanings of an informational text
b. draw inferences from informational text
c. determine the textual evidence that supports an analysis of the informational text

The goal of an informational text is to state facts, or create interpretations of them. Discerning these views is essential to create a fuller understanding of the piece, which you can then guide your students towards. Your students should learn a few key tactics for discerning meaning from an informational text. They should read slowly and closely, taking in all manner of details, instead of skimming to the parts that appearing most interesting. They should take notes (usually on a piece of scratch paper, though plenty of writers insist noting in the margins is perfectly acceptable as long as the book is yours).

And they should be prepared to summarize. Summarizing will allow the key textual points of interest to float to the top. If a summary is incomplete, that means key evidence was missing. Likewise, if a summary is too long, then some of the details included weren't necessary. Ask yourself, can this summary be trimmed down and still retain its meaning? If the answer is yes, it contains superfluous detail.

Inferring from the text is another essential skill. Students must be taught to follow "clues" that lead to less obvious information. A multitude of clues pointing in the same direction strengthens the inference. Contradictory clues weaken it, or refute it entirely. For example, if a story is set in France but does not explicitly say so, students might infer this from the presence of French names like Jacques or Matilde, or from references to French landmarks.

Students should be required to refer directly to the text when making inferences. Direct quotes or close paraphrases only. An inference is not a random guess.

SKILL I.B.2 **Understands how a variety of organizational text structures and patterns can be used to develop a central idea in informational texts.**

a. identify the central idea of an informational text

b. analyze how an author develops or refines a central idea in informational text

c. identify the organizational pattern of an informational text (e.g. problem-solution, cause-effect, sequence order)

d. analyze how ideas are connected and distinguished from one another in an informational text

e. identify how text features (e.g. index, glossary, headings, footnotes, visuals) contribute to the central idea of an informational text

The central idea of an informational text is almost always presented towards the beginning of the piece. The author wants you to understand what they're discussing early on. To do otherwise is unclear writing. Sometimes it's stated directly in the title, other times the central idea is developed further in a topic sentence or introductory paragraph, which should provide a preview of the ideas to come.

The idea is then further developed through supporting evidence. In more complex writings, this evidence is often deeply personal, and is buried under layers of editorializing or poetic detail. Students should become adept at parsing personal opinion from objective fact, while still not downplaying the role opinions play in good informational writing.

Keywords to look for in informational texts are transitional terms like "furthermore" or "thus". These are a common and effective way to separate ideas in a piece, to determine which idea follows naturally from the previous one.

Informational texts are also sometimes deepened by textual features like glossaries, footnotes, or indexes. These provide the reader with technical knowledge they might not otherwise possess, and removes the need for them to do superfluous research. Glossaries make searching for specific terms easier, and footnotes are usually used to expand on a point.

**SKILL
I.B.3**

Understands how textual evidence supports interpretations of an informational text.
a. distinguish between connotation and denotation in an informational text
b. identify how technical language is used in an informational text
c. distinguish between what the text says explicitly and what is inferred from the text

Good informational writing is fine-tuned, whether by committees of people or the author and editor, to convey a specific opinion or piece of data. The differences in word choice can have a massive effect on this.

To begin, you must understand the difference between "connotation" and "denotation". A denotation has an explicit meaning. "Smart" and "intelligent" and "genius" all essentially mean the same thing. The denoted meaning is that the person described is very mentally acute.

Connotations are implied meanings, and they depend largely on context. "Run" and "sprint" both describe the action of moving quickly, but "sprint" connotes a more harried, athletic, or even panicked kind of movement. Likewise, "yummy" and "delicious" have different connotations; yummy is more informal, almost childish, and can speak to the intelligence or familiarity of the person doing the describing.

Technical language is often inaccessible to the layperson, and some more advanced informational texts won't define their terms for you. It is important to be able to infer from context what technical terms mean. For instance, you might not know what an apiary is, but if the rest of the text describes the housing habits of bees, you can eventually discern it is a term for a beehive.

**SKILL
I.B.4**

Understands the rhetorical strategies writers use to convey purpose and perspective in informational texts.
a. determine an author's point of view or purpose in an informational text
b. analyze how an author uses rhetoric to support a point of view and/or purpose in an informational text
c. recognize rhetorical strategies (e.g. satire, irony, understatement, hyperbole)

Strictly informative writing is boring. The mind wanders when confronted with a list of naked facts. Thus, writers employ rhetoric to embolden their work, to better communicate thought, mood, or information to the reader and bring them closer to their point of view. Rhetoric is also useful for determining a writer's point of view on a topic, which could strengthen or weaken their claim, and even reveal overt bias or manipulation of facts.

Here are a few of the more common rhetorical strategies:

Satire – the use of irony, humor, exaggeration or mockery to expose failings of logic, especially in the context of politics or other social systems. Satire is a broad genre, encompassing overt parodies like Jonathan Swift's *A Modest Proposal*, which straight-facedly suggests the best way to deal with the poor is to cook and eat them, or more nuanced cultural critiques, such as *Gulliver's Travels* by the same author, which tells the fantastic tale of a man who journeys to a land of tiny humans to explore deeper social commentary about the inherent "smallness" of political and religious conflict.

Hyperbole – A common aspect of satire is hyperbole, wherein the author adopts a perspective they disagree with and push it to an absurd conclusion, thereby highlighting the perspective's failings. A famous example is Machiavelli's *The Prince*, which criticizes the very notion of nobility and statism by espousing the idea that all rulers should strive to be as feared as possible. Like many works of satire, *The Prince* is often interpreted more literally, its hyperbole lost on the kinds of people it criticizes, and thus the term "Machiavellian" exists to describe rulers who unironically agree with its satirical principles.

Understatement – Something of an opposite to hyperbole, understatement highlights the negative aspects of something by minimizing them. Understatements are usually humorous, delivering a layer of engaging absurdity to a thought. Some examples might include the phrases "World War II was a bit messy" or "Adolph Hitler was not very nice".

Irony – Another broad concept, irony in rhetoric is the use of words to convey the opposite meaning than their literal definition. Satire is often built on ironic rhetorical flourishes, and the above examples express this. When one talks about Hitler, one expects passionate denouncement of his ideals and actions. Communicating instead that he was "not very nice" subverts this expectation, and creates irony. Irony is also employed in dramatic storytelling; the Ancient Greeks employed irony in their tragedies, most famously in *Oedipus Rex*, where the titular character's downfall is brought about when he kills his father and marries his mother as the prophecy foretold, despite insisting that these things would never come to pass.

Polemic – A polemic is a passionate attack, a rant, a diatribe against someone or something. Polemics can employ the above rhetorical devices, and are usually characterized by their intensity. George Orwell famously polemicized against fascism in his works.

Allegory – Wherein a narrative is created with a direct hidden meaning, often a political or moral one. Orwell's *Animal Farm* is ostensibly a tale about farm animals rising up against their human rulers, but it contains many direct references to the rise of the fascist party in Russia.

SKILL I.B.5 — **Understands the method authors use to appeal to a specific audience.**

a. identify methods of appeal or persuasion (e.g. expert opinion, generalization, testimonial)
b. evaluate the effectiveness of an author's methods of appeal
c. understand how technical or non-technical language is used to appeal to a targeted audience

---

Authors must know their audience so that they might connect with them on a deeper level. Authors who write for everyone write for no one. It's important to focus on a specific group of people to maximize the effect your words will have.

When writing informatively, authors must straddle the line between sharing their expertise in a technical and authoritative manner, and still appeal to laypeople. If an author is writing for a more advanced audience, they will be more comfortable using technical terms without explanation. For newer readers, they will need to define their terms or risk alienating their readers.

In the case of journalists or other outside observers, they will rely on the expertise of an interview subject to enhance their work. This is called a testimonial – a formal statement endorsing someone or something. Depending on the qualifications of the subject, this can be extremely effective or destroy the point entirely. An endorsement from the President of the United States can be very impressive. An endorsement from a gas station worker, perhaps less so.

Likewise, the author's expertise must be considered. Do they rely on generalizations, or do they dig deeper into their topic? All of this affects the strength of informative writing.

SKILL I.B.6 **Understands how authors develop and support a written argument.**
a. evaluate the argument and specific claims in a text
b. determine the author's purpose and evaluate the author's reasoning
c. evaluate whether evidence is relevant, factual, or significant
d. identify false statements and fallacious reasoning (e.g. slippery slope, red herring, straw man, post hoc ergo propter, etc.)

When you've determined what an author's perspective is, as well as their central thesis, the next step is assessing the argument's merits.

First, determine if the argument being made is factually-based, or more opinion-based. Most informational writing has a mixture of the two, though some technical works in the "hard science" categories like math or biology will impart universal truths that require little editorializing. Observe the author's claims. They should be stated clearly in the thesis towards the front of the work. Does the evidence support this conclusion? You might need to do external research to know for sure.

There are a few fallacious arguments that you can spot even in works on topics you're unfamiliar with. Logical fallacies are universal, and while they might not necessarily disprove an entire argument through their mere presence, they do not bode well for the author's authority on the subject.

Here are some of the most common logical fallacies:

Appeal to authority – Essentially, the idea that if an important or smart figure says it, it must be factually true. Someone's qualifications can certainly improve their authority on a subject and lend their opinions more weight, but this does not determine that what they say is true.

Slippery slope – This fallacy contends that if one negative thing occurs, it will inevitably lead to other negative effects down the line. Unless each of these effects is proven to be causally connected to the first event, this argument should be considered invalid.

Straw man – To "straw man" an argument is to argue with its weakest form, to hyperbolize, summarize, or otherwise alter an argument into an absurd interpretation before addressing it. It occurs when one debates with a conception of an argument, rather than the argument, itself. If one person argues that the environment must be protected and the second person responds with "You just want to destroy businesses!" then the second person has straw-manned the first.

Hasty Generalization – A conclusion drawn with incomplete or misinterpreted evidence. For example, if someone hears that cities with more Chinese restaurants have more fires, they might assume (incorrectly) that Chinese restaurants cause fires.

This also reveals the distinction between correlation and causation, which is essential for understanding an argument. A causal connection is a proven, replicable result. A correlation is an association between two data points that may not be causal. In the above example, one possible explanation is that Chinese restaurants cause fires, but this is incorrect – larger cities tend to be more international, and thus have more ethnic food options. And larger cities have more fires than smaller ones. Thus, the cities with more Chinese restaurants have more fires. The two data points are correlated, but there are not causally connected.

Post hoc ergo propter hoc – A complicated name for an assumption that if even A occurred before event B, then event A must have caused event B. For instance, you eat a sandwich and become sick. Did the sandwich make you sick? It's possible, but without more facts it cannot be taken for a certainty.

Circular argument – Wherein an argument proves itself. "The Bible is infallible because it is the word of God, and it is undoubtedly the word of God because this is stated infallibly in the Bible".

Ad hominem – An attack on a person's character rather than the merit of their arguments. Like the Appeal to Authority, a speaker's expertise can certainly factor in to the weight of their claims, but the lack of total mastery of a subject, or the presence of unrelated absurd or irrational opinions, do not in of themselves invalidate a point. Neil Degrasse Tyson might not be an economist, but his opinions on the economy should be refuted with better information, not a mere statement that he is unqualified.

> **SKILL I.B.7** **Knows how to interpret media and non-print texts and how they will influence an audience.**
> a. evaluate multiple sources of information presented in different media or formats
> b. determine persuasive techniques used in different media

People, especially younger media consumers, have a tendency to trust anything they see on the news. It is essential for teachers to give their students the critical thinking skills they require to parse through media bias and determine the facts for themselves.

Students should never receive all of their news from one source. Even if the source is thoroughly vetted and factually sound, it will still present some form of bias, or at least a perspective that can limit the scope of what they report on. All news outlets focus on news interesting to people in the same geographic location, which will inevitably lead to news in the wider world going underreported. Similarly, some news outlets exhibit overt political views that can color or distort events. Even if one happens to agree with these views, it can affect their intake of factual information and skew their perception of the world.

News anchors are trained to be neutral, to deliver reportage in clear tones with minimal inflection or editorializing. Nonetheless, opinion pieces are rapidly becoming mixed in with "straight news", and news anchors have allowed their personal opinions to color their reportage. There are various body language cues one can spot that can color a piece of news as untrustworthy or editorialized – sighs, laughs, eye rolls, tears, or even overt expressions of shock or outrage from the reporter. A certain degree of editorial slant appears in all news, but one must be aware of it if they are to find the objective, factual core.

News organizations will also sometimes give extra coverage to one story while downplaying another. They can do this to appeal to certain audiences for increased viewership, or sometimes in an attempt to build a narrative, intentionally or otherwise. For instance, a news organization might give extra attention to one political candidate's tastes in food, while downplaying another candidate's recent corruption scandal. Intentionally or no, this skews public perception of one candidate over the other, and should be criticized, even if you happen to support the candidate who benefits.

DOMAIN II
LANGUAGE USE AND VOCABULARY

SECTION II
LANGUAGE USE AND VOCABULARY

SKILL II.1	Knows major works and authors of United States, British, World (including non-Western), and young adult literature.

a. explain the function of the different parts of speech
b. identify errors in standard English grammar, usage, syntax, and mechanics (e.g., inconsistent verb tense, non-parallel structure, sentence fragments, run-ons)
c. justify grammar, usage, syntax, and mechanics choices (e.g., colon versus semicolon, its versus it's, saw versus seen, etc.)
d. identify different components of sentences (e.g., clauses, phrases)
e. identify different structures of sentences (e.g., simple, complex, compound)

Root, Base, and Compound Words

Structural elements within words can be used independently to determine meaning. Often including a historical element, root words commonly stem from Latin or Greek origins. Base words are considered language in the simplest form. Compound words create meaning through the combination of two words that are able to stand alone.

Root words: A root word is a word from which another word is developed. The second word can be said to have its "root" in the first. This structural component lends itself to an illustration of a tree and its roots, which can concretize the meaning for students. Typically, root words cannot stand alone.

Aquatic (aqua = water)
Submerge (sub = under)
Junction (junct = connect)

Base words: Unlike root words, base words are stand-alone linguistic units that cannot be deconstructed or broken down into smaller words. Prefixes and suffixes are connected to base words to create meaning.

Retell (base = tell)
Instructor (base = instruct)
Sampled (base = sample)

Compound words: Compound words occur when two or more base words are connected to form a new word. The meaning of the new word is in some way connected to the meanings of the base words.

> Everything (every + thing)
> Backpack (back + pack)
> Notebook (note + book)

Prefixes and Suffixes

Prefixes are beginning units of meaning that can be added (affixed) to the beginning of a base word or root word. They are also known as bound morphemes, meaning that they cannot stand alone as words.

Prefix	Meaning	Example
Re-	To do again	Reread
Anti-	Against	Anticlimactic
Uni-	One	Unibrow
Mis-	Incorrect	Misunderstood

Suffixes are ending units of meaning that can be affixed to the end of a base word or root word. Suffixes transform the original meanings of base and root words. Like prefixes, they are also known as bound morphemes because they cannot stand alone as words.

Suffix	Meaning	Example
-able	Ability	Likeable
-er	One who	Teacher
-less	Without	Careless
-est	Comparative	Smartest

Inflectional endings are types of suffixes that impart a new meaning to the base word or root word. These endings change the gender, number, tense, or form of the base or root word. Just like other suffixes, these are bound morphemes.

Ending	Original Word	New Word
-s	Road	Roads
-es	Mix	Mixes
-ing	Write	Writes
-ed	Sample	Sampled

Connotation and Denotation

Denotation is the literal meaning of a word, as opposed to its connotative meaning. *Connotation* refers to the implications and associations of a given word, distinct from the denotative or literal meaning. Connotation is used when a subtle tone is preferred. It may stir up a more effective emotional response than if the author had used blunt, denotative diction. For example, "Good night, sweet prince, and flights of angels sing thee to thy rest," a line from Shakespeare's Hamlet, refers to a departure or death; connotatively, it renders the harsh reality of death in gentle terms such as those used in putting a child to sleep.

Informative connotations are definitions agreed upon by the society in which the learner operates. A skunk is "a black and white mammal of the weasel family with a pair of pineal glands which secrete a pungent odor." (denotative) The Merriam-Webster Collegiate Dictionary adds that this odor is also "offensive." The color, species, and glandular characteristics are informative. The interpretation of the odor as offensive is affective (connotative).

Affective connotations refers to the personal feelings a word arouses. A child who has no personal experience with a skunk and its odor will feel differently about the word "skunk" than a child who has smelled the spray of a skunk or been conditioned to associate offensiveness with it. The fact that our society views a skunk as an animal to be avoided will affect the child's interpretation of the word. In fact, it is not necessary for one to have actually seen a skunk (that is, have a denotative understanding) to use the word in either connotative expression. For example, one child might call another child a skunk, connoting an unpleasant reaction (affective use) or, seeing another small black and white animal, call it a skunk based on the definition (informative use).

Grammar is the proper usage of words and phrases. For tests such as the AP English Literature and Composition and AP English Language and Composition, it is critical to demonstrate proper use of grammar and avoid errors in usage, spelling, diction, and rhetoric.

Multiple choice questions will test your knowledge of a variety of English grammar rules: parts of speech, syntax, sentence types, sentence structure, sentence combining, phrases and clauses, modifiers, and capitalization.

Writing prompts will give you an opportunity to showcase your knowledge of these rules. Patterns of error in the written sections will immediately result in a lower grade. You will want to be sure to avoid sentence fragments and run-on sentences. Recognition of sentence elements necessary to express a complete thought, proper use of independent and dependent clauses, and proper punctuation will correct such errors. Reviewing the following grammar points will assist in getting higher scores for both multiple choice and essay questions.

Parts of Speech

There are eight parts of speech: nouns, verbs, adjectives, adverbs, pronouns, conjunctions, prepositions, and interjections.

Noun: A person, place or thing. (student, school, textbook)
Verb: An action word. (study, read, run)
Adjective: Describes a verb or noun. (smart, beautiful, colorful)
Adverb: Describes a verb. (quickly, fast, intelligently)
Pronoun: Substitutes for a noun. (he, she, it)
Conjunction: Joins two phrases. (because, but, so)
Preposition: Used before nouns to provide additional details. (before, after, on)
Interjection: Expresses emotion. (Ha!, Hello!, Stop!)

Syntax

Although widely different in many aspects, written and spoken English share a common basic structure or syntax (subject, verb, and object) and the common purpose of fulfilling the need to communicate—but there, the similarities end.

Spoken English follows the basic word order mentioned above (subject, verb, object) as does written English. We would write as we would speak: "I sang a song." It is usually only in poetry or music that that word order or syntax is altered: "Sang I a song."

Types of Sentences

Sentence variety is a great way to demonstrate your knowledge of the various sentence types in the writing portions for the AP English exam.

Sentence Types

Declarative	Makes a statement	I bought a new textbook
Interrogatory	Asks a question	Where did you buy it?
Exclamatory	Expresses strong emotion	I can't believe it!
Imperative	Gives a command	Put it on the table

Clauses are connected word groups that are composed of at least one subject and one verb. (A subject is the doer of an action or the element that is being joined. A verb conveys either the action or the link.)

subject   verb
Students are waiting for the start of the assembly.

               subject   verb
At the end of the play, students waited for the curtain to come down.

Clauses can be *independent* or *dependent*. Independent clauses can stand alone or can be joined to other clauses, either independent or dependent. Words that can be used to join clauses include the following:

- for
- and
- nor
- but
- or
- yet
- so

Dependent clauses, by definition, contain at least one subject and one verb. However, they cannot stand alone as a complete sentence. They are structurally dependent on an independent clause (the main clause of the sentence). There are two types of dependent clauses: (1) those with a subordinating conjunction and (2) those with a relative pronoun.

Coordinating conjunctions include the following:

- although
- when
- if
- unless
- because

Example: Unless a cure is discovered, many more people will die of the disease. (dependent clause with coordinating conjunction [unless] + independent clause)

Relative pronouns include the following:
- who
- whom
- which
- that

Example: The White House has an official website, which contains press releases, news updates, and biographies of the president and vice president. (independent clause + relative pronoun [which] + relative dependent clause)

Sentence Structure

You must recognize simple, compound, complex, and compound-complex sentences. Use dependent (subordinate) and independent clauses correctly to create these sentence structures.

Simple: Joyce wrote a letter.
Compound: Joyce wrote a letter and Dot drew a picture.
Complex: While Joyce wrote a letter, Dot drew a picture.
Compound/complex: When Mother asked the girls to demonstrate their newfound skills, Joyce wrote a letter and Dot drew a picture.

Note: Do not confuse compound sentence elements with compound sentences.

Simple sentence with compound subject: Joyce and Dot wrote letters.

The girl in row three and the boy next to her were passing notes across the aisle.

Simple sentence with compound predicate: Joyce wrote letters and drew pictures.

The captain of the high school debate team graduated with honors and studied broadcast journalism in college.

Simple sentence with compound object of preposition: Coleen graded the students' essays for style and mechanical accuracy.

Parallelism

Recognize parallel structures using phrases (prepositional, gerund, participial, and infinitive) and omissions from sentences that create the lack of parallelism.

Prepositional phrase/single modifier:
Incorrect: Coleen ate the ice cream with enthusiasm and hurriedly.
Correct: Coleen ate the ice cream with enthusiasm and in a hurry.
Correct: Coleen ate the ice cream enthusiastically and hurriedly.

Participial phrase/infinitive phrase:

Incorrect: After hiking for hours and to sweat profusely, Joe sat down to rest and
　　　drinking water.

Correct: After hiking for hours and sweating profusely, Joe sat down to rest and drink
　　　water.

Recognition of Misplaced and Dangling Modifiers

Dangling phrases are attached to sentence parts in such a way that they create ambiguity and incorrectness of meaning.

Participial phrase:

Incorrect: Hanging from her skirt, Dot tugged at a loose thread.

Correct: Dot tugged at a loose thread hanging from her skirt.

Infinitive phrase:

Incorrect: To improve his behavior, the dean warned Fred.

Correct: The dean warned Fred to improve his behavior.

Prepositional phrase:

Incorrect: On the floor, Father saw the dog eating table scraps.

Correct: Father saw the dog eating table scraps on the floor.

Particular phrases that are not placed near the word they modify often result in misplaced modifiers. Particular phrases that do not relate to the subject being modified result in dangling modifiers.

Error: Weighing the options carefully, a decision was made regarding the punishment
　　　of the convicted murderer.

Problem: Who is weighing the options? No one capable of weighing is named in the
　　　sentence. Thus, the participle phrase "weighing the options carefully" dangles.
　　　This problem can be corrected by adding a subject of the sentence who is
　　　capable of doing the action.

Correction: Weighing the options carefully, the judge made a decision regarding the
　　　punishment of the convicted murderer.

Error: Returning to my favorite watering hole brought back many fond memories.

Problem: The person who returned is never indicated, and the participle phrase
　　　dangles. This problem can be corrected by creating a dependent clause from
　　　the modifying phrase.

Correction: When I returned to my favorite watering hole, many fond memories came
　　　back to me.

Recognition of Syntactical Redundancy or Omission

These errors occur when superfluous words have been added to a sentence or key words have been omitted from a sentence.

Redundancy
Incorrect: Joyce made sure that when her plane arrived that she retrieved all of her luggage.
Correct: Joyce made sure that when her plane arrived she retrieved all of her luggage.
Incorrect: He was a mere skeleton of his former self.
Correct: He was a skeleton of his former self.

Omission
Incorrect: Dot opened her book, recited her textbook, and answered the teacher's subsequent question.
Correct: Dot opened her book, recited from the textbook, and answered the teacher's subsequent question.

Avoidance of Double Negatives

This error occurs from positioning two negatives that cancel each other out (creates a positive statement).

Incorrect: Dot didn't have no double negatives in her paper. Dot didn't have any double negatives in her paper.

Spelling

Spelling rules are extremely complex, based as they are on rules of phonics and letter doubling, and are replete with exceptions. Even adults who have a good command of written English benefit from using a dictionary. Adolescent students will also benefit from learning how to use a dictionary and thesaurus.

Most plurals of nouns that end in hard consonants or hard consonant sounds followed by a silent e are made by adding s. Some nouns ending in vowels only add s.

fingers, numerals, banks, bugs, riots, homes, gates, radios, bananas

Nouns that end in the soft consonant sounds s, j, x, z, ch, and sh add es. Some nouns ending in o add es.

dresses, waxes, churches, brushes, tomatoes, potatoes

Nouns ending in y preceded by a vowel just add s.

boys, alleys

Nouns ending in y preceded by a consonant change the y to i and add es.

babies, corollaries, frugalities, poppies

Some noun plurals are formed irregularly or are the same as the singular.

sheep, deer, children, leaves, oxen

Some nouns derived from foreign words, especially Latin, may make their plurals in two different ways, one of them anglicized. Sometimes the meanings are the same; other times, the two plurals are used in slightly different contexts. It is always wise to consult the dictionary.

appendices, appendixes
criterion, criteria
indexes, indices
crisis, crises

Make the plurals of closed (solid) compound words in the usual way except for words ending in -ful, which make their plurals on the root word.

timelines, hairpins, cupsful

Make the plurals of open or hyphenated compounds by adding the change in inflection to the word that changes in number.

fathers-in-law, courts-martial, masters of art, doctors of medicine

Make the plurals of letters, numbers, and abbreviations by adding s.

fives and tens, IBMs, 1990s, ps and qs (Note that letters are italicized.)

Capitalization

Capitalize all proper names of persons (including specific organizations or agencies of government); places (countries, states, cities, parks, and specific geographical areas); things (political parties, structures, historical and cultural terms, and calendar and time designations); and religious terms (any deity, revered person or group, or sacred writing).

Percy Bysshe Shelley, Argentina, Mount Rainier National Park,
Grand Canyon, League of Nations, the Sears Tower, Birmingham,
Lyric Theater, Americans, Midwesterners, Democrats, Renaissance,
Boy Scouts of America, Easter, God, Bible, Dead Sea Scrolls, Koran

Capitalize proper adjectives and titles used with proper names.

California Gold Rush, President John Adams, Senator John Glenn

Some words that represent titles and offices are not capitalized unless used with a proper name.

Capitalized	Not capitalized
Congressman McKay	the congressman from Florida
Queen Elizabeth	the queen of England
Commander Alger	the admiral
President George Washington	the president

SKILL II.2 **Understands the use of affixes, context, and syntax to determine word meaning.**
a. apply knowledge of affixes to determine word meaning
b. use context clues to determine word meaning
c. apply knowledge of syntax to determine word meaning
d. analyze nuances of word meaning and figures of speech

While **syntax** includes the rules for the structure, or word order, in a sentence, semantics dictates the meaning. Looking at the syntax can make language almost seem like a math problem. There's a specific order of operations in order to form a sentence. You may remember sentence mapping from your early English classes, which taught how to write a sentence that includes a subject and a predicate. Creating a diagram for your sentences identifies the verb, subject, and object.

The meaning behind writing can be shifted in a number of deliberate ways. **Semantics** can include letters or symbols in writing, and when read aloud, meaning can be conveyed using hand gestures, pauses, and facial expressions. Thinking in terms of punctuation, adding two or three exclamation points to the end of a sentence is going to express a much more emotional message when compared to a simple period, or even one exclamation mark.

Also referred to as a register, regional and social **dialects** vary in class, social structure, and geographic location. Even within one language, we have hundreds, if not thousands, of variations in the way we speak. These outside influences have an impact on the vocabulary that we use, the pronunciation, and even the speed in which we talk. For example, the plural phrase for you in the South is referred to as "y'all," which is seldom heard in other parts of the country. Someone native to the Northeast may refer to a Pepsi as a "soda," where others may call it "pop." Accents also vary within our country and across the globe for the English language. Ireland, England, and Australia are very unique in their pronunciation of words, and you may have a hard time speaking to someone with a very strong accent. It is difficult to determine what an "American" accent may sound like, as geographic factors play a large role in differentiating regions to their own unique accents.

See also Skill 1.A.8

SKILL II.3

Understands the use of print and digital reference materials to support and enhance language usage.

a. determine the most appropriate digital or reference material (spellchecker, style manual, dictionary, glossary) for a particular language usage task

As technology becomes more and more integrated into the classroom, the teacher must serve not only as an educator, but as a curator of the kinds of media their students are exposed to. Mass communication brings incredible opportunities for information to spread, but misinformation can spread just as quickly. And print media still plays a vital role. It's important for the teacher to weed out counter-factual sources and guide their students towards the research tools they can best understand.

Researchers identify four main types of vocabulary: reading, listening, speaking, and writing. The lexicons for each of these vocabularies can vary wildly. Surely you've seen a word in print you couldn't recognize when spoken, or have terms you use in a paper that you'd never use in conversation with friends. It's important for teachers to understand their students are acquiring vocabulary for each of these subsets.

Most language acquisition occurs organically. The student does not even realize they are learning new words as they listen to their parents discuss the weather, or having a Dr. Seuss book read to them, or watch commercials on TV. All of these modes of communication can influence the growth of the "listening" vocabulary, but in the Digital Age, where even the youngest of us spend much of their day reading Facebook statuses or YouTube comments, the reading vocabulary is undergoing something of a golden age as the written word becomes a dominant force.

For classroom purposes, teachers must strive to keep their students' digital content grammatically and syntactically sound. Lazy text speak might suffice for adults making weekend plans, but students must be educated more formally. Schools have databases for approved academic content for their students to peruse, and numerous free resources exist online to aid teachers in their curricula.

Consider the principles of a Universal Design for Learning (UDL) classroom. UDL specifies that a good lesson plan offers multiple avenues for students to engage with the material, such as visual, aural, or textual methods of learning.

According to Reif (1993), students retain 10% of what they read, 20% of what they hear, 30% of what they see, 50 % of what they see AND hear, 70% of what they say, and 90% of what they say and do. UDL uses technology in the classroom to cover as many of these bases as possible.

Consider using different kinds of media as you create your lesson plan. A video, a podcast, a reading by the teacher, a reading by the students. Variety will keep them engaged and ensure all types of learners are catered to.

Likewise, encourage the students to make use of print resources. Despite the numerous benefits of digital press, engagement drops when on a computer due to the variety of distractions available. A student who wants to learn a new word should be made, on occasion, to look it up in a print dictionary. The labor of opening the book, rifling through the pages, finding the word and reading the definition will promote retention. You should also encourage students to use thesauri for the same reason. Spell-checking software has lessened the burden on many writers, but it can't replace an innate understanding of English spelling norms. And style guides promote dialogue about the aspects of "proper" English that students can engage and even argue with.

SKILL II.4	Is familiar with the variations in dialect and diction across regions, cultural groups, and time periods.
	a. understand the concept of dialect and its appropriateness depending on purpose and audience

"Dialect" refers to the regional or cultural variations in a specific language. It is distinct from an accent – accent refers to the mode of speaking, the pace, timbre, and vocal posture of the sounds being made, whereas dialect also involves vocabulary and syntax. In short, dialect is what you say and how you say it. Every language develops unique dialects as it grows in usage, and oftentimes these dialects become distinct enough that they effectively become languages of their own. Dialects must be mutually comprehensible to be considered united within a language, but try telling that to the Minnesotan desperately trying to get directions from a gas station attendant in rural Louisiana.

As a teacher, it is important to straddle the line between offering "standard" or "correct" English, both as a subject being taught and as a mode of communicating, while also acknowledging and utilizing dialectical variations for the benefit of the students. The goal of language is communication, not "correctness". And though the teacher must strive to standardize their material as much as possible, to ignore the dialectical variations in English both fails to prepare students for the types of communication they must use, and risks being culturally insensitive.

In American English, the chief dialects you're likely to encounter are:
- Standard English
- African American Vernacular English (AAVE, or "ebonics")
- East Coast/ New England
- Mid-Atlantic
- Midland
- Southern
- Various urban dialects, such as Chicago, New York City, or Bostonian accents
- Less common though still prevalent are the Canadian and British dialects of English

A student who speaks an unfamiliar dialect will sometimes prefer to listen at first while they can absorb the modes of speech of their classmates. It's important to respect this adjustment period, and to be gentle and encouraging with any corrections that must occur. Many students can develop insecurities due to their dialects – AAVE, for instance, is often maligned as an "incorrect" mode of speech, and students who use it may struggle to adjust their speech patterns to what is acceptable from their peers, even if the dialect is encouraged with their friends and family at home. Thus, many students resort to "code-switching", or speaking different dialects for different occasions. We all do this to some degree, speaking formally with our bosses and informally with our friends, but to students still acquiring language, this can be a source of bullying or identity crisis. One also runs the risk of being insensitive in attacking this dialect too forcefully. All dialects are deeply tied with social class, education level, and in America, race. "White" modes of speech are often viewed as superior to "black" ones, even if both dialects subvert grammar norms and accomplish the primary goal of being understood.

As such, teachers should find fascination in the methods their students use to speak. Dialect is a natural part of language acquisition, and can be something to take pride in. Regional qualifiers like "y'all" might not be ideal in a formal written essay, but in spoken communication, they allow students to expand their vocabulary in intellectually stimulating ways.

> **SKILL II.5**
>
> **Knows commonly used research-based approaches for supporting language acquisition and vocabulary development for diverse learners.**
> a. eecognize examples of commonly used research-based strategies for language acquisition and vocabulary development
> b. wvaluate the effectiveness of specific strategies to support language acquisition and vocabulary development
> c. interpret research and apply it to particular instructional challenges related to language acquisition and vocabulary development

The science of teaching is constantly evolving, and educators must keep abreast of new developments in the field. English learners come from all backgrounds, from wealthy and educated families to lower-class immigrants with little knowledge of the culture they're entering. Certain research-based strategies can be tailored to fit the needs of all these students, expediting the learning process and easing the burden on the teacher. Praxis requires you to demonstrate knowledge of some common research-based teaching methods, and to gauge the efficacy of newer methods as they appear.

Here are three common forms of research-based education for English learners:
- Explicit Teaching
- Providing Practice
- Adjusting Language of Instruction

Explicit teaching is overt and teacher-led. The teacher models how to solve a problem for the class using clearly defined items in the curricula, going step-by-step through the process and explaining their reasoning along the way. Goals must be clearly defined, and connections to already-acquired knowledge are essential. The teacher must frequently ask questions of the students to monitor their engagement and retention, and to steer them towards the correct answers if they should stray. Teachers must also be cautious not to over-explain. The students must draw their own connections and make their own mistakes, within reason. If the goals and curricula are clearly defined, and the information is clearly supported by previous knowledge the students have acquired, the students will begin to realize their own mistakes before they need to be pointed out.

Providing practice is exactly what it sounds like. Students require many and varied opportunities to practice their newly-acquired language skills. Teachers can minimize the risk for their students by engaging in choral response exercises, or by working with them in smaller groups where mistakes won't embarrass them. If properly guided, students will seek to practice these skills in their own ways. Teachers should allow this process to happen organically whenever possible, and can help facilitate these scenarios with peer-tutoring sessions or group activities. The more the students communicate with each other, the more they will practice without realizing it. There are also numerous games, puzzles, or online resources students can use that will allow them to practice their new skills while also having fun.

Adjusting instructional language ensures that students will comprehend and retain what they're told in class. Depending on skill and development level, students can become baffled by overly technical language. The teacher must be careful to make their lesson accessible, while still modeling ideal modes of communication.

When introducing a new concept, use clear, explicit language. Ambiguity will only confuse students. Clearly identify the goals for each lesson, and use markers like "first, second, and third" when outlining the curriculum. Be consistent in your language – repetition helps emphasize important concepts the students need to retain.

SECTION III
WRITING, SPEAKING, AND LISTENING

SECTION III
WRITING, SPEAKING, AND LISTENING

Understands the distinct characteristics of various modes of writing (e.g., informative, argumentative).
a. distinguish between common modes of writing (e.g., argumentative, informative/explanatory, narrative)
b. identify examples of common types within modes of writing (e.g., journal, letter, essay, speech, blog)
c. determine which mode is the most appropriate for an author's purpose and audience

Expository and Persuasive Essay

When teaching students to write an expository or persuasive essay, audience and purpose must be determined. A preliminary review of literature is helpful. For example, if the topic is immigration, a cursory review of the various points of view in the debate going on in the country will help the writer decide what this particular written piece will try to accomplish. The purpose could be to review the various points of view, which would be an *informative purpose*. On the other hand, the writer might want to take a point of view and provide proof and support with the purpose of changing the reader's mind. The writer might even want the reader to take some action as a result of reading. Another possible purpose might be simply to write a description of a family of immigrants.

Once a cursory review has been completed, it is time to begin research in earnest and to prepare to take notes. If the thesis has been clearly defined and some thought has been given to what will be used to prove or support this thesis, a tentative outline can be developed. A thesis plus three points is typical. However, less importance is now given to this "formulaic" five-paragraph structure in an essay. Instead, writing that is organized and possesses a strong voice is what really matters.

Decisions about introduction and conclusion should be deferred until the body of the paper is written. Note-taking is much more effective if the notes are being taken to provide information for an outline. With this purpose in mind it is less likely that the writer will go off on time-consuming tangents when taking notes.

Formal outlines inhibit effective writing. However, a loosely constructed outline can be an effective device for note-taking that will yield the information for a worthwhile statement about a topic. Sentence outlines are better than topic outlines because they require the writer to do some thinking about the direction a subtopic will take.

Once this preliminary note-taking phase is over, the first draft can be developed. The writing at this stage is likely to be highly individualistic. However, successful writers tend to just write, keeping in mind the purpose of the paper, the point that is going to be made, and the information that has been turned up in the research. Student writers need to understand that this first draft is just that—the first one. It takes more than one draft to write a worthwhile statement about a topic. This is what successful writers do. It can be helpful to have students read the various drafts of a story by a well-known writer.

Once the draft is on paper, a stage that is sometimes called revision occurs. Revision is rereading objectively, testing the effectiveness on a reader of the arrangement and the line of reasoning. The kinds of changes that will need to be made are rearranging the parts, changing words, adding information that is missing but necessary, and deleting information that doesn't fit or contribute to the accomplishment of the purpose.

Once the body of the paper has been shaped to the writer's satisfaction, the introduction and conclusion should be fashioned. An introduction should grab the reader's interest and perhaps announce the purpose and thesis of the paper unless the reasoning is inductive. In this case purpose and thesis may come later in the paper. The conclusion must reaffirm the purpose in some way.

Narrative Writing

It seems simplistic, yet it's true: The first and most important measure of a story is the story itself. *The story's the thing.* However, a good story must have certain elements and characteristics.

Plot is the series of events, involving conflict, that make up the story. Without conflict there is no story, so determining what the conflicts are should be a priority for the writer. Once the conflicts are determined, the outcome of the story must be decided. Who wins? Who loses? What factors go into making one side of the equation win out over the other? The pattern of the plot is also an important consideration. Where is the climax going to occur? Is denouement necessary? Does the reader need to see the unwinding of all the strands? Many stories fail because a denouement is needed but not supplied.

Characterization, the choice the writer makes about the devices he or she will use to reveal character, requires an understanding of human nature and the artistic skill to convey a personality to the reader. This is usually accomplished subtly through dialogue, interior monologue, description, and the character's actions and behavior. In some successful stories, the writer comes right out and tells the reader what this character is like. However, sometimes there will be discrepancies between what the narrator tells the reader about the character and what is revealed about the character, in which case the narrator is unreliable, and that unreliability of the voice on which the reader must depend becomes an important and significant device for understanding the story. (See also Skill 1.2 Characterization)

Point of view is essentially the eyes through which the reader sees the action. It is a powerful tool not only for the writer but also for the enjoyment and understanding of the reader. The writer must choose among several possibilities: first-person narrator objective, first-person narrator omniscient, third-person objective, third-person omniscient, and third-person limited omniscient.

The most common point of view is the third-person objective. If the story is seen from this point of view, the reader watches the action, hears the dialogue, and reads descriptions and must deduce characterization from all of these. In third-person objective, an unseen narrator tells the reader what is happening, using the third-person pronouns: *he, she, it, they*. The effect of this point of view is usually a feeling of distance from the plot.

More responsibility is on the reader to make judgments than in other points of view. However, the author may intrude and evaluate or comment on the characters or the action.

The first-person narrator is also a common point of view. The reader sees the action through the eyes of a character in the story who is also telling the story. In writing about a story that uses this voice, the writer must analyze the narrator as a character. What sort of person is he or she? What is this character's position in the story—observer, commentator, or actor? Can the narrator be believed, or is he or she biased? The value of this voice is that, while the reader is able to follow the narrator around and see what is happening through that character's eyes, the reader is also able to feel what the narrator feels. For this reason the writer can involve the reader more intensely in the story itself and move the reader by invoking feelings—pity, sorrow, anger, hate, confusion, disgust, etc. Many of the most memorable novels are written in this point of view.

Another narrative voice often used may best be titled "omniscient" because the reader is able to get into the mind of more than one character or sometimes all the characters. This point of view can also bring greater involvement of the reader in the story. By knowing what a character is thinking and feeling the reader is able to empathize when a character feels great pain and sorrow, which tends to make a work memorable. On the other hand, knowing what a character is thinking makes it possible to get into the mind of a pathological murderer and may elicit horror or disgust.

Style, the unique way a writer uses language, is often the writer's signature. The reader does not need to be told that William Faulkner wrote a story to know this because his style is so distinctive that his work is immediately recognizable.

The writer must be cognizant of his or her own strengths and weaknesses and continually work to hone the way sentences are written, words are chosen, and descriptions are crafted until they are razor sharp. The best advice to the aspiring writer is to read the works of successful writers. If a writer wants to write a best-seller, then the writer needs to be reading best-sellers.

ORGANIZATIONAL STRUCTURES

Authors use a particular organization to best present their concepts. Teaching students to recognize organizational structures helps them to understand authors' literary intentions and to decide which structure to use in their own writing.

Cause and Effect: When writing about why things happen as well as *what* happens, authors commonly use the cause and effect structure. For example, when writing about how he became so successful a CEO might talk about the specific events leading up to his success. The events are the *causes* that lead to the *effect*, or result, of him becoming a wealthy and powerful businessman.

Compare and Contrast: When examining the merits of multiple concepts or products, compare and contrast lends itself easily to organization of ideas. For example, a person writing about foreign policy in different countries will put the policies against each other to point out differences and similarities, a structure that easily highlights the concepts the author wishes to emphasize.

Problem and Solution: This structure is used in many handbooks and manuals. Information organized around procedure-oriented tasks, such as a computer repair manual, gravitates toward a problem and solution format because it offers a clear, sequential text organization.

Transitions

To help students identify and evaluate the structure of the text teach them to examine the transitions that are used. Have them evaluate their effectiveness.

Introduction and Conclusion

In addition to the organization students should examine the introduction and the conclusion. Examine the opening by asking such questions as "How does it begin?" "How does the writer pull you in?" "Why does it begin the way it does?"

Examine the closing by asking "Is the closing effective?" "What impression does it leave you with?" "Why?"

SKILL III.2	**Understands how awareness of task, purpose, and audience contribute to effective writing.**

a. identify how the task, purpose, and intended audience affects a piece of writing

b. choose the most appropriate type of writing for a task, purpose, or audience

c. evaluate the effectiveness of a piece of writing for a task, purpose, or audience

Teachers must always be aware of the purpose of each piece of writing they present to a class. Are you trying to inform? To challenge? To provoke discussion? Whether you're using original worksheets you've created yourself, or assigning readings from a classic work of literature, you should have clear goals in mind for your students to fulfill.

Likewise, students must develop their own instincts about how to alter their work for a specific task. If they are writing to inform, their prose must be explicit and authoritative. Prevaricating, begging the question, and passive language should be discouraged. Students should also be encouraged to state their intent in the opening paragraph.

SKILL III.3	**Understands the characteristics of clear and coherent writing (supporting details, organization, conventions etc.).**

a. identify details that develop a main idea

b. organize a text clearly and coherently

c. use varied and effective transitions throughout a text

d. justify stylistic choices within a clear and coherent piece of writing

e. introduce, develop, and conclude a text effectively

Students must be taught structured writing. Our increasingly interconnected world relies largely on informal writing, with texts, Tweets, or Facebook statuses occupying much of our time. But students must be expected to learn the fundamentals of English before they can be allowed to break them.

The core of the student writing experience is the five-paragraph essay. Teachers use this method to communicate the basics of structured writing to students in a way that's easy to understand (and easy to grade). A five-paragraph essay traditionally follows this formula:

- An introductory paragraph that outlines the thesis of the piece, with a topic sentence or "hook", three or four lines of supporting evidence, and a closing sentence that emphatically states what the writer is trying to prove
- Three paragraphs of supporting evidence, which expand on the topics outlined in the introductory paragraph.
- A closing paragraph, which summarizes the previous arguments and restates the now-proven thesis.

The five-paragraph essay offers students a way to develop their instincts in regards to structure, voice, and thesis. The relatively constrained formula of the essay frees them to focus on other writing mechanics, such as transitions – students should be expected to vary their transitional phrases ("First off", "Secondly", "Furthermore", etc.) to increase readability and flow. Stylistic variations in the essay are certainly allowed, but they must be justified by the thesis. Florid language or complex syntax can distract from the message of the piece. The five-paragraph essay encourages lean, concise writing.

Since the supporting evidence in a five-paragraph essay is clearly highlighted, this also allows the teacher to determine how effective the students were at making their point. If a piece of evidence isn't relevant, it can be clearly pointed out to the student so they can fix it in a redraft. Likewise, if a student can't fully support their argument, they should be encouraged to try a new overall tactic.

Introductions and conclusions are relatively simple in a five-paragraph essay. The introduction must state what the student intends to prove, and the conclusion should illustrate what has been proven. Students will come to understand the value in supporting their arguments, and these rudiments will carry over into more complex, less rigidly structured forms of writing.

SKILL III.4

Understands effective and ethical research practices, including evaluating the credibility of multiple print and digital sources, gathering relevant information, and citing sources accurately.
a. identify relevant information during research on a given topic
b. evaluate the credibility of a print or digital source
c. identify effective research practices (e.g. formulating a question, narrowing or broadening a topic, choosing effective resources)
d. identify the components of a citation
e. cite source material appropriately
f. integrate information from source material to maintain the flow of ideas

The teacher must always be able to parse through bad research and misinterpreted facts to give their students the clearest information possible. You will need to demonstrate an understanding of what constitutes good and bad research for the Praxis exam, looking at examples of both and stating your reasons for choosing one example over another.

Research must be concise and logical. Even minor flaws in reasoning call the efficacy of the entire endeavor into question. Keep an eye out for vague terms, unsupported conclusions, or flaws in methodology. Any sample groups should be representative of larger groups, not selectively chosen to push a particular result. And variables must be controlled whenever stated, or else clearly marked as uncontrollable. Good research states its goals clearly and is supported with clear evidence. It should never leave you guessing.

Seek out vetted research on topics that are supported by repeated experimentation. Individual reports of discrepant events might be exciting, but they shouldn't be presented to a classroom as anything other than a curiosity until their results can be duplicated. If multiple sources report the same result in an experiment, the research is stronger. If a lone team accomplished a result once and never again, other factors likely tainted the outcome.

Also, accept that any experiment will have limitations. Good research reports will acknowledge these. Rarely does educational science deal in strict absolutes. Good research contains clearly cited references to the works it builds off. The American Psychological Association (or APA) uses the most common citation format. Here is an example:

Author, J. (1990) *Title: Subtitle Etc.* Chicago, IL. University of Chicago Press.

These citations can frequently give you more sources to pull from as you build your lesson plans.

SKILL III.5

Understands components of effective speech and presentation delivery.
a. identify characteristics of effective delivery of a speech or presentation (e.g., eye contact, visual aids, tone)
b. evaluate the advantages and disadvantages of using different media to present ideas
c. determine whether information is present clearly, concisely, and logically

Students should employ visual or multimedia aids in their presentations. This promotes engagement with the material, as the information can be absorbed both visually and aurally (or perhaps using other senses). Posters, videos, slideshows, music, or what have you, are good examples. As long as it serves the presentation and provides relevant information without becoming distracting, it should be commended. Similarly, students must project good body language while they speak. No slouching or shifting from foot to foot. They should stand up tall, speak clearly, and even employ hand gestures or vocal fluctuations to emphasize important points.

Some methods of presentation are best suited to specific topics and ideas. Music, for instance, has the disadvantage of being difficult to talk over. The audience's attention can be divided between hearing the music and hearing the speaker, and if the speaker chooses to stop talking so the audience can listen, they risk losing the attention of the audience as well. Unless the presentation is on music itself, music is a risky inclusion. Similarly, slideshows can organize and present information effectively, but students often simply repeat the information that's in the slideshow without actually adding to it. Students must be required to make sure that if they choose to include a component in their presentation, be it speaking, visual aids, or props, they are using that tool to its fullest potential.

SKILL III.6

Knows approaches for instructing students in the effective use of digital media to support and enhance communication.
a. identify techniques for instructing students to choose and use technological tools (e.g. presentation software, blogs, wikis) for effective communication
b. evaluate the effectiveness of specific technology-based strategies to achieve enhanced understanding of communication goals

There has been a sharp increase in the past few decades in the use of technology in the classroom. Teachers are rapidly becoming aware of the myriad uses for websites like YouTube or the various educational apps and programs that can enrich their students' education experience.

A few caveats exist, however. Technology is inherently distracting. Students, especially younger ones, will quickly become enamored with a computer screen and lose focus on what the teacher is saying. Expect to become background noise when you let the students start using computer apps. Prepare for this. If your lesson plan is well-structured and the goals are clearly laid out, students will still accomplish their lesson requirements. But try to establish these things before you turn them loose on their devices, or else everything you say will be lost in the clatter of keyboards.

Remember also, students may grow up around technology and be very familiar with how to operate it, but that doesn't mean they can use tech effectively for learning purposes. Using a mouse and keyboard is second nature to the newer generation, but they still require structured lessons and critical thinking skills to better educate themselves. Don't confuse facility for inquiry.

Another way to better maintain the focus of your lessons is to center the lesson around one piece of technology, such as a digital whiteboard or projector. The rule of tech stealing a student's focus still applies here – students will become more engaged with the material if it's presented to them in a multimedia display. And if your screen is the only one operating in the class, you have a monopoly on their attention.

Spend some time early in the session to go over some of the fundamentals of all our current iterations of tech. Teach the students how to save a file, search a hard drive, login to an account, create a safe password, and the rudiments of commonly used programs like Microsoft Word. Always use a program yourself before handing it off to your students, and set clear time goals and plans for collecting work.

> **SKILL III.7 Understands commonly used research-based approaches to teaching components of writing.**
> a. recognize commonly-used research strategies (e.g. modeling, writing workshop) for teaching components of the writing process
> b. identify research based strategies for teaching particular writing tasks
> c. interpret research and apply it to particular writing instruction challenges

Writing is not a solitary activity. In the classroom, students must be taught how to brainstorm, structure their work, formulate arguments, and share their work with an audience. The teacher can facilitate this process with several research based methods. A few of the most common are listed below:

Modeling writing strategies – Teachers should lay down the basics of the writing process step by step, engaging students to think creatively and methodically. Model steps such as brainstorming, outlining, creating a thesis, adding supporting details, and editing or redrafting the work once it's done. Teachers can also demonstrate how to use spell check or word processing software to expedite this process, but due attention should also be given to freehand techniques, such as editor's shorthand symbols.

Group writing – Students that directly engage with each other during the writing process will begin to challenge each other. They will discover the counterarguments that may arise in their discourse, which will strengthen their overall points. Writing does not happen in a vacuum. This will also allow students to assess the clarity in their own works and determine if they're being understood. If the students are at the same skill level, they will sometimes make similar mistakes, which the teacher should step in to correct.

Collaborative writing can be done in large groups or in small partnerships. Students can be encouraged to brainstorm ideas as a class, then write their own pieces, and share them again at class end. You can also pair off students and have them trade essays for editing purposes, to better establish the collaborative nature of writing.

Summarizing text – Students should be made to summarize the works they read to demonstrate comprehension of the text. This also serves to teach them the value of clear and succinct writing, and how to assess which details are most essential to retain when describing something.

Close reading – Similarly, students must form clear understandings of any assigned reading they encounter in school. The students' interpretation of a piece is not so essential as how they support that interpretation. They should be made to directly quote or summarize sections of the piece to support their arguments, and any writing they do on this interpretation should be emphatic and authoritative. Encourage them to look at a work literally and symbolically, to question the author's choices and assess what devices they employed to better tell their tale. If a student did not enjoy a work (a common occurrence), ask them how they would have done it better. This can open up avenues of communication with your students and help them engage with material they find interesting.

Goal-setting – Writing takes myriad forms, but it's important for the teacher to shrink focus. As such, create a structured curriculum with clear, incremental goals for the students to accomplish. Longer papers with larger page counts are a start, but also judge students by the merit of their arguments – by their supporting details, their transitions, their comprehension of a comparable work or the depth of their research. Students must be pushed outside their comfort zones if they are to grow as learners.

SKILL
III.8
Understands purposes and methods of assessing reading, writing, speaking, and listening.
a. recognize a variety of research based approaches to and purposes of formative and summative assessment of reading, writing, speaking, and listening (e.g. use of rubrics, conferencing techniques, providing useful feedback)
b. evaluate the effectiveness of research-based approaches to, and purposes of, formative and summative assessment of reading, writing, speaking, and listening

Once students are motivated to write, the time must come to grade them. Writing is a dense and varied art form, but for classroom purposes, certain rubric must be adhered to in order to standardize student work and ensure everyone is graded fairly.

There are five main factors you must judge in every student's work: content, fluency, conventions, vocabulary, and syntax.

Fluency refers to the student's ability to translate their thoughts into words. Young students will struggle initially to create coherent sentences as they develop an attention span, as well as the fine motor skills necessary for the act of writing.

Content describes the actual thoughts being presented. One must assess content along the lines of accuracy, organization, and cohesion. Ask yourself, are the arguments clear? Is there a good topic sentence? Do supporting points logically follow the main thesis? Does the piece stay on topic or does it stray?

Conventions determine a piece's readability. This is where the nuts and bolts of writing come into play – the grammar, spelling, capitalization, punctuation, and other formatting details a student must follow. Spell-checking programs handle much of this process now, but the teacher must still be cognizant of issues like word choice or sentence structure.

When judging syntax, look for variation in syntactical models. A series of "First I did this then. Then I did that. Then I did something else" quickly tries the reader's patience. Students must be encouraged to vary their work, so they can communicate effectively. Sentence length also factors into this step. Complex sentences should be rewarded (assuming they are coherent).

Vocabulary, likewise, should be judged by students' willingness to experiment. Early learners are prone to modifiers like "really tired" and "very big", so the teacher should encourage them to branch out into stronger words like "exhausted" and "enormous". Nothing is quite as rewarding as watching a student play with a new word!

SKILL III.9 Understands the components of effective oral communication in a variety of settings (e.g., one-on-one, in groups).

a. identify a variety of techniques (e.g. selecting age-appropriate topics, facilitating appropriate discussion behavior, ensuring accountability) to ensure productive participation and active listening in collaborative discussions

b. evaluate the effectiveness of specific strategies for students initiating and participating effectively in discussions

Public speaking is an art, one that students must learn over the course of their educational life. As a teacher, part of your job is to push students outside their comfort zone and give them the rudiments of public speech and presentation that they'll need to rely on later in life.

Students should be encouraged to speak clearly and loudly when talking in front of the class. Diction is a necessity. Diction is the style of enunciation a public speaker must use to communicate effectively with a group. Good diction requires them to pronounce each syllable clearly, to hammer consonant sounds and avoid slurring or glossing over words and phrases. They must also maintain good volume while they speak. Not only will this make students easier to understand from the back of the class, but it will lend their presentation more authority and make their arguments more agreeable.

When students work in small groups or partnered up, care must be taken to ensure they stay on topic. Students will naturally gravitate towards their friends, but it's not necessary to split them up unless this becomes a problem.

SKILL III.10 Knows that students bring various perspectives, cultures, and backgrounds to reading, writing, listening, and speaking, and how to incorporate that awareness into instruction.

a. use knowledge of students individual and group identities to plan instruction responsive to their needs

b. know strategies for creating a safe environment for reading, speaking, writing, and listening

The difference between students of two separate backgrounds can be vast. Social class or monetary status, for instance, has a huge effect on the vocabulary a student can be expected to possess. Students from lower class families can absorb less than half the vocabulary from their home life as students from wealthier backgrounds. As such, great care must be taken to ensure all students are equally cared for in the classroom.

Bullying along these lines can be detrimental to education and the mental health of the students and must be dealt with firmly. Students should find fascination in their backgrounds, not things to mock. Show-and-tell exercises can help bridge this gap by letting students bring a piece of their home life into the classroom. It doesn't have to be a physical object – stories about parents' jobs, or favorite holiday memories, or talks about family history can help open up avenues of communication about students' backgrounds. This can also prompt genuine inquiry into somewhat divisive topics, like religion or cultural backgrounds. But try to do your research first. A student with a rough home life may not be comfortable sharing.

SAMPLE TEST

SAMPLE TEST

Section I: Essay Test

Several prompts are given. You are expected to exhibit a variety of writing skills. In most testing situations, you will have thirty minutes to respond to each of the prompts. For some tests you will be allowed sixty minutes, either to incorporate more than one question or for greater preparation and editing time. Read the directions carefully and organize your time wisely.

Section II: Multiple-Choice Test

This section contains 130 questions. In most testing situations, you will be expected to answer from 35 to 40 questions within 30 minutes. If you time yourself on the entire battery, take no more than 90 minutes.

Section III: Answer Key

Section IV: Answer Key with Rationales

Section I: Essay Prompts

Prompt A

Write an expository essay discussing effective teaching strategies for developing literature appreciation with a heterogeneous class of ninth graders. Select any appropriate piece(s) of world literature to use as examples in the discussion.

Prompt B

After reading the following passage from Aldous Huxley's *Brave New World*, discuss the types of reader responses possible with a group of eight graders.

> He hated them all—all the men who came to visit Linda. One afternoon, when he had been playing with the other children—it was cold, he remembered, and there was snow on the mountains—he came back to the house and heard angry voices in the bedroom. They were women's voices, and they were words he didn't understand; but he knew they were dreadful words. Then suddenly, crash! something was upset; he heard people moving about quickly, and there was another crash and then a noise like hitting a mule, only not so bony; then Linda screamed. 'Oh, don't, don't, don't!' she said. He ran in. There were three women in dark blankets. Linda was on the bed. One of the women was holding her wrists. Another was lying across her legs, so she couldn't kick. The third was hitting her with a whip. Once, twice, three times; and each time Linda screamed.

Section II: Multiple-Choice Test

TOTAL – 130 Multiple Choice Questions
TIME – 150 Minutes

1. **In classic literature, which of the following do NOT represent the function of a character?**

    A. Embody an idea

    B. Embody an ideal acting in the world

    C. Examine social conditions

    D. Present the setting

2. **Mrs. Samuels is wondering how she might best draw her seventh grade class into reading more deeply into the text as they begin their next novel study. Which of the following writing exercises would best contribute to critical reading skills?**

    A. Summarizing each paragraph as it is read.

    B. Doing a reflection on the chapter, connecting it to their own lives.

    C. Discussing the chapter in small groups.

    D. Drawing a scene from the book into a journal.

3. **Which of the following does not involve critical thinking?**

    A. Fill in the blank tests

    B. Summarizing

    C. Reflective essays

    D. Prediction of outcomes

4. **Mr. Trundle would like to do a close reading of the novel, The Outsiders, but isn't sure how to begin. Mrs. Smith meets with him to discuss the benefits of using New Criticism for the close reading. Which of the following will promote New Criticism close reading?**

    A. Taking notes while the teacher reads the text out loud.

    B. Learning about the author's overall intentions

    C. The setting and time in which the author wrote the work

    D. The literary text itself.

5. **Which of the following literary theories, is based on moral and ethical teachings?**

    A. Structuralism

    B. New Criticism

    C. Moral Criticism

    D. Psychoanalytic Criticism

6. **Which literary theory focuses on the inner workings and motivations of a character's actions?**

    A. Moralism

    B. Deconstruction

    C. Marxism

    D. Psychoanalytical Criticism

7. **Mrs. Godwin has been reading about UDL (universal design for learning) and wants to create a lesson plan that would incorporate what she has learned. Which of the following characteristics would be inherent in a good UDL lesson plan?**

   A. Multiple avenues for students to interact with the material

   B. Worksheets that ask students to read the passage several times

   C. Listening to the teacher read the material, then taking a test

   D. Removing all technology and distractions from the classroom

8. **According to Reif (1993) when students are presented with material, which of the following will result in the greatest retention of material?**

   A. Reading the material

   B. Seeing a skill performed

   C. Saying and doing a skill

   D. Hearing and seeing a skill

Questions 9-16. Read the following selection and answer the questions below, selecting the best choice of the options presented.

Two roads diverged in a yellow wood,
And sorry I could not travel both
And be one traveler, long I stood
And looked down one as far as I could
To where it bent in the undergrowth;

Then took the other, as just as fair,
And having perhaps the better claim,
Because it was grassy and wanted wear;
Though as for that the passing there
Had worn them really about the same,

And both that morning equally lay
In leaves no step had trodden black.
Oh, I kept the first for another day!
Yet knowing how way leads on to way,
I doubted if I should ever come back.

I shall be telling this with a sigh
Somewhere ages and ages hence:
Two roads diverged in a wood, and I—
I took the one less traveled by,
And that has made all the difference.

9. **Who wrote this poem?**

   A. Robert Frost

   B. Emily Dickinson

   C. John Keats

   D. Emily Bronte

10. **When the author uses the phrase "wanted wear" in the third stanza, what does that mean?**

   A. It looked just as fair as the other path.

   B. It was not as inviting.

   C. The path didn't go the same way as the other one.

   D. The path was less traveled than the other one.

11. The author says that he "took the one less traveled by"; what does that mean?

    A. The other path looked like it was used more.

    B. He did the right thing when others chose the wrong one.

    C. He took the one on the left.

    D. He took the one on the right.

12. What is another way the author states his path was the "one less traveled by"?

    A. "both that morning equally lay"

    B. "no step had trodden black"

    C. "Somewhere ages and ages hence"

    D. "having perhaps the better claim"

13. What does the author imply since he took the path less traveled?

    A. He has run into fewer people that try to bully him into doing what they want.

    B. Life is tougher getting to see the light.

    C. He was sorry he didn't chose to go the more well-trod path.

    D. His life is better for choosing to go his own path.

14. What is the rhyme scheme?

    A. ABBAB

    B. ABABA

    C. ABAAC

    D. ABAAB

15. Taking the road less traveled by made all the difference because _____.

    A. the decision shaped his life

    B. it was a good hike

    C. the character was able to find peace

    D. he created a new path on the road

16. What literary device is used in this poem?

    A. Personification

    B. Propaganda

    C. Paradox

    D. Parallelism

17. Mr. Date notices that Emil, a new student from India, who has for the last few months been very quiet, has suddenly begun speaking with others in the classroom. While Mr. Date is glad that the others have accepted him, he notices that Emil is adjusting his speech patterns from correct English to non-standard English. He is worried that Emil will not learn to speak English correctly. In the preceding scenario, what is the behavioral action that Emil is engaged in, called?

    A. Code-switching

    B. Peer integration

    C. Ebonics

    D. Colloquialism

18. **Ms. Heisel prefers to show her class of English learners how to solve a problem, going step by step through the process, offering explanations along the way. Her method of teaching is which of the following?**

    A. Adjusting language of Instruction

    B. Explicit Teaching

    C. Providing Practice

    D. Goal oriented practice

19. **Which of the following illustrates the benefits of the five paragraph essay formula?**

    A. Allow students to expand on topics with detail

    B. Utilizes outside sources

    C. Offers a way to develop instincts about structure

    D. Teaches the importance of a thesis statement

20. **When grading students' essays, which of the following can cause flaws in reasoning which calls into question the efficacy of the entire essay?**

    A. Weak thesis statements

    B. Poor handwriting

    C. Misspelled words

    D. Unsupported conclusions

21. **Mr. Kirk wants to start using the computer lab more with his lower quartile students, but isn't sure what the best approach will be. Which of the following would work best to accomplish this goal?**

    A. Prepare a structured lesson plan with clear goals.

    B. Give students a long list and plenty of time to finish it.

    C. Make sure they all use headsets, to minimize distraction.

    D. Establish discipline and the rules before starting the project.

22. **What is one of the primary benefits of group writing?**

    A. Those that understand the process can assist those who are lagging.

    B. Students that are directly engaged with each other during the writing process will begin to challenge each other.

    C. Students will internalize structure.

    D. Students who work with others often learn new vocabulary words, and will incorporate them into their essays.

23. One of the problems young writers have with the writing process is that the elaboration on a topic sentence is often lacking. Understanding this, Ms. Kenyon wants to use a research based approach to directly build up this skill. Which of the following would be the best choice for developing elaboration and supportive details in an essay?

    A. Group writing

    B. Modeling

    C. Summarizing text

    D. Close reading

24. Which of the following activities does NOT fall under the category of collaborative writing practices?

    A. Computer based essay writing

    B. Brainstorming ideas

    C. Sharing their writing out loud

    D. Working in pairs

Questions 25-32. Read the following selection and answer the questions below, selecting the best choice of the options presented.

"I went to work the next day, turning, so to speak, my back on that station. In that way only it seemed to me I could keep my hold on the redeeming facts of life. Still, one must look about sometimes; and then I saw this station, these men strolling aimlessly about in the sunshine of the yard. I asked myself sometimes what it all meant. They wandered here and there with their absurd long staves in their hands, like a lot of faithless pilgrims bewitched inside a rotten fence. The word 'ivory' rang in the air, was whispered, was sighed. You would think they were praying to it. A taint of imbecile rapacity blew through it all, like a whiff from some corpse. By Jove! I've never seen anything so unreal in my life. And outside, the silent wilderness surrounding this cleared speck on the earth struck me as something great and invincible, like evil or truth, waiting patiently for the passing away of this fantastic invasion.

—*Heart of Darkness*

25. **Who wrote this novel?**

    A. Joseph Conrad

    B. James Joyce

    C. Jane Austen

    D. Charles Dickens

26. **What does the following line represent?**

    "I saw this station, these men strolling aimlessly about in the sunshine of the yard."

    A. Soldiers enjoying their day

    B. Men being unaware of the negativ,ity that surrounds them

    C. Positivity is infectious

    D. The station is a happy place

27. **What does the word staves mean?**

    A. Machete

    B. Axe

    C. Gun

    D. Wooden club

28. **What does the ivory represent?**

    A. Death

    B. Prosperity

    C. Jewelry

    D. Trade

29. **What literary device is used when describing the ivory?**

    A. Alliteration

    B. Allegory

    C. Simile

    D. Personification

30. **What does rapacity represent?**

    A. Greed

    B. Rapid movement

    C. Intelligent

    D. Generous

31. **What literary device is used in this passage?**

    "And outside, the silent wilderness surrounding this cleared speck on the earth struck me as something great and invincible, like evil or truth, waiting patiently for the passing away of this fantastic invasion."

    A. Simile

    B. Metaphor

    C. Illusion

    D. Onomatopoeia

32. **Which style of writing is represented in this novel?**

    A. Biographical

    B. Autobiographical

    C. Expository

    D. Persuasive

33. **Which of the following is NOT one of the main factors that should be judged in every student's work?**

    A. Content

    B. Fluency

    C. Handwriting

    D. Syntax

34. Ms. Gonzalez notices that Alisha, a new student who is from Pakistan, is having a difficult time fitting in. Which of the following is a good way to promote integration without focusing the attention directly on Alisha?

    A. Discussing family holidays and traditions.

    B. Studying Pakistan and asking Alisha about it

    C. Reading a story from Pakistan

    D. Having Alisha teach some phrases in her native language to the students

35. Mr. Lawrence is grading some of his class's summaries and is feeling overwhelmed. While his students have completed the assignment, they have written longer than necessary paragraphs. How might he instruct his students on paring down their summaries?

    A. Have one of the students who has done it correctly, to be the teacher for the day.

    B. Show the students a sample summary that is correct.

    C. Ask them to write the main idea, only.

    D. Model the revision process, showing students how to determine the necessity of some details.

36. Which of the following is a key transitional word to look for in informational texts written by students?

    A. Well

    B. So

    C. Furthermore

    D. Then

37. Mr. Reeder's eighth grade class has been invited to join Mrs. Kirby's ninth grade class to go see a performance of Romeo and Juliet at the local community college. To prepare for the field trip, they should:

    A. Read an abbreviated version of the play and study listening skills

    B. Read a few important sections from the play to become familiar with Shakespearean language and style

    C. Assign the play to be read as a homework assignment

    D. Read a synopsis of the play in class and discuss

38. The Montgomery County High School English Department has decided to implement learning strategies that would encourage students to create student led reading communities. Which would be the best way to begin this process?

   A. One set day a week each class would bring a book or magazine in and read for that class period.

   B. The class brainstorms as a group, suggesting books that they would like to share with the class, or study as a novel unit.

   C. Book reports are studied, and assigned.

   D. Each student contributes a book to the in-class library.

39. Which of the following is NOT a rhetorical writing strategy?

   A. Satire

   B. Hyperbole

   C. Irony

   D. Theme

40. Mr. Cline has a lower quartile literature class of seniors. Which of the following teaching strategies would work best for motivating them to engage with the work more?

   A. Allow group work, interactive panel discussions, portfolio creation, and many opportunities for hands-on applications.

   B. Allow students to select from a list which readings they would like to study.

   C. Practice 'popcorn' reading using an anthology

   D. Assign a list of vocabulary words

Questions 41-47. Read the following selection and answer the questions below, selecting the best choice of the options presented.

"Finished, it's finished, nearly finished, it must be nearly finished. Grain upon grain, one by one, and one day, suddenly, there's a heap, a little heap, the impossible heap. I can't be punished any more. I'll go now to my kitchen, ten feet by ten feet by ten feet, and wait for him to whistle me. Nice dimensions, nice proportions, I'll lean on the table, and look at the wall, and wait for him to whistle me."

—*Endgame*

41. Who wrote this play?

   A. Anton Chekov

   B. William Shakespeare

   C. Lillian Hellman

   D. Samuel Beckett

42. **What literary device is used throughout this passage?**

    A. Simile

    B. Metaphor

    C. Euphemism

    D. Repetition

43. **What does the impossible heap represent**

    A. Life's greatest hurdles

    B. A pile of grain so tall it cannot be moved

    C. Death

    D. A mountain

44. **The whistle symbolizes _____ .**

    A. A referee

    B. The character's father

    C. Death

    D. An angel

45. **What is an endgame?**

    A. The final play in a game, such as chess

    B. The end of a negotiation

    C. A wish

    D. None of the above

46. **What is the author trying to portray in this selection?**

    A. An old man

    B. A prisoner

    C. A farmer

    D. A mill worker

47. **What best describes this selection?**

    A. Epic

    B. Foreshadowing

    C. Cliffhanger

    D. Flashback

48. **In an informative essay, which of the following should NOT be included in the introductory paragraph?**

    A. An attention getting device

    B. A general introduction to the topic

    C. Details that support the main idea of the essay

    D. A thesis statement

Questions 49-55. Read the following passage carefully before you decide on your answers to the questions.

O wild West Wind, thou breath of Autumn's being,
Thou, from whose unseen presence the leaves dead
Are driven, like ghosts from an enchanter fleeing,

Yellow, and black, and pale, and hectic red,
Pestilence-stricken multitudes: O thou,
Who chariotest to their dark wintry bed

The winged seeds, where they lie cold and low,
Each like a corpse within its grave, until
Thine azure sister of the Spring shall blow

Her clarion o'er the dreaming earth, and fill
(Driving sweet buds like flocks to feed in air
With living hues and odors plain and hill:

Wild Spirit, which art moving everywhere;
Destroyer and preserver; hear, oh, hear!

Thou on whose stream, 'mid the steep sky's commotion,
Loose clouds like earth's decaying leaves are shed,
Shook from the tangled boughs of Heaven and Ocean,

Angels of rain and lightning: there are spread
On the blue surface of thine aery surge,
Like the bright hair uplifted from the head

Of some fierce Maenad, even from the dim verge
Of the horizon to the zenith's height,
The locks of the approaching storm. Thou dirge

Of the dying year, to which this closing night
Will be the dome of a vast sepulchre,
Vaulted with all thy congregated might

Of vapors, from whose solid atmosphere
Black rain, and fire, and hail will burst: oh, hear!

49. **The first line of this poem exhibits what poetic devices?**
   I.   Alliteration
   II.   Personification
   III.   Onomatopoeia

   A. Only I

   B. Only II

   C. Only III

   D. I and II

50. **What best describes the final stanza of this selection?**

   A. Slant rhyme

   B. Heroic couplet

   C. Hyperbole

   D. Irony

51. **"Wild Spirit, which art moving everywhere; Destroyer and preserver; hear, oh, hear!"**

   This passage displays a...

   A. Enjambment

   B. Slant rhyme

   C. Simile

   D. Iamb

52. **This poem is written in what style?**

   A. Vers libre

   B. Heroic couplet

   C. Epic saga

   D. Iambic pentameter

53. What in the poem is compared to "Angels of rain and lightning"?

    A. The wind

    B. Maenads

    C. Clouds

    D. Human souls

54. "Of the dying year, to which this closing night/ Will be the dome of a vast sepulchre,/ Vaulted with all thy congregated might"

    This passage exhibits…

    A. A metaphor

    B. An allegory

    C. A comparison

    D. An allusion

55. How many stanzas does this poem contain?

    A. Four

    B. Five

    C. Eight

    D. Ten

56. Which is the most important issue to be aware of when utilizing computer based writing of essays?

    A. The writer can tend to focus only on completing the task, rather than spending time on the supportive details.

    B. The technology makes it very easy to make corrections quickly, and removes the facet of contemplation from the writing process.

    C. The proofreading function does not allow students to catch their own mistakes and fix them.

    D. The print looks so clean and clear that students do not see their mistakes.

Use the following introduction from a student essay for the following questions.

(1) When reading this poem it is clear that there are two stories going on. (2) First, it is a story of a man finding an ancient statue half buried in the sands. (3) The traveler who finds the statue comes away with a new way to view life, in general, and so does the reader. (4) This poem is the author's way of showing that time does not respect anything manmade, that it is all temporary and can go away to be forgotten.

57. In the sample essay, which of the sentences provides the thesis?

    A. Sentence 1

    B. Sentence 2

    C. Sentence 3

    D. Sentence 4

58. **Which of the sentences in the provided sample provide detail?**

    A. Sentence 1

    B. Sentence 2

    C. Sentence 3

    D. Sentence 4

59. **Which of the following is NOT a common logical fallacy?**

    A. Appeal to Authority

    B. Slippery Slope

    C. Exposition

    D. Straw man

60. **Many junior high school students have trouble distinguishing between correlation and causation. A lack of understanding about these two distinct properties can lead to poor persuasive writing, because the essence of an argument is not understood. Which of the following would lay the groundwork for better persuasive essay writing?**

    A. Purposely writing false correlations as a class

    B. Analyzing short scenarios for false correlations and causations

    C. Discussing the definitions of correlation and causation

    D. Read about false correlations on the internet

61. **Of the following statements, which is most true in regards to expository essays?**

    A. Summative evaluations work best when scoring.

    B. Should always be formal

    C. Should incorporate other forms of discourse when providing elaboration

    D. This type of essay writing is exclusive to other forms of discourse.

62. **When evaluating the media, what does the appearance of sighs, laughs, eye rolls, tears, or even overt expressions of shock or outrage from the reporter, indicate about news that is being delivered?**

    A. That the news is colored by the personal opinions of the reporters.

    B. That the news is trustworthy.

    C. That the news is opinion based and not fact based

    D. That the news station is trying to push their own agenda

63. **Media bias is an important topic to a contemporary audience. In order to discuss and teach a unit on this subject, what of the following is a good activity?**

    A. Giving a lecture on the topic.

    B. Having a reporter come to speak to the class

    C. Watch a newscast that features two political candidates and analyze how it is presented.

    D. Hand out a worksheet about media bias, then have students watch the nightly newscast to analyze it.

64. **Which of the following statements is incorrect in regards to media in the classroom?**

    A. The internet makes it possible for students to reach beyond their own regional culture and location to connect with others on a global scale.

    B. Educational media can make certain topics more powerful when utilized correctly.

    C. Virtual reality experiences provide students a chance to experience information unavailable to them in their current circumstance.

    D. Teachers should be judicious in their use of media in the classroom, due to the saturation of students by media at home.

65. **Of the following statements, which statement about multimedia in the classroom offers a specific goal?**

    A. Teachers can engage their students by offering opportunities to foster a critical perspective toward audiovisual presentations.

    B. Students who listen to an audio book have less interaction than those who simply read the passages themselves.

    C. Reading text engages students to think more deeply about what it is they are reading.

    D. Mental images are formed when an audio message/book is listened to.

66. **Which of the following statements is not a fallacy in logic?**

    A. All students in Ms. Sanders' class have failed a grade. Misha is in Ms. Sanders' first period. Misha has failed a grade.

    B. All students who have failed a grade are in Ms. Sanders' class. Misha is in Ms. Sanders' first period class. Misha has failed a grade.

    C. Misha has failed a grade. Misha is in Ms. Sanders' first period class. All students in Ms. Sanders' first period class have failed a grade.

    D. If Misha has failed a grade, then she is a grade ahead. Misha is in Ms. Sanders' class. Misha has not failed a grade.

67. **Mr. Hill's 10th grade class wants to create a webcast about the devastation of Hurricane Matthew, and utilize some multimedia in their creation of the webcast. Which of the following would be the best choices for making the presentation more effective?**

    A. A PowerPoint slideshow with before and after photos.

    B. Music clips from the devastated areas, both before and after the hurricane.

    C. Video footage of the devastation as well as the rebuilding efforts

    D. Interviews of different officials in the area, as well as those affected by the storm.

68. **Of the following issues, which would not be as much of an issue with an oral presentation?**

    A. Making sure the purpose for the presentation is clear.

    B. Needing to know the audience's particular tastes and proclivities

    C. Creating a Powerpoint slide to correspond with each point

    D. Creating the content to fit the specific occasion.

69. **Of the following writing techniques, which would allow students to improve the cohesion of the ideas in a persuasive essay?**

    A. Key transitional words that show relationship between one idea to another

    B. Using conjunctions to link ideas

    C. Using quotes to offer validity

    D. Increasing the amount of adjectives and adverbs to make the detail more vivid

70. **Use the following statements to answer the following question:**

    The teachers at NM High are confident in their ability to teach English at a high level. Staff at NMHS always welcome new ideas for presenting the material.

    In order to show contrast between these two ideas in a persuasive essay, which of the following transition words would be the best insertion?

    A. The teachers at NMHS are confident in their ability to teach English, and always welcome new ideas for presenting material.

    B. Because the teachers at NMHS are confident, they welcome new ideas.

    C. When the teachers at NMHS are confident about their abilities, they welcome new ideas.

    D. NMHS English teachers and staff are confident in their ability to teach at a high level; however, they also welcome new ideas for presenting material.

Questions 71-78. Read the following passage carefully before you decide on your answers to the questions.

William Wordsworth — "I Wandered Lonely As A Cloud"

I wandered lonely as a cloud
That floats on high o'er vales and hills,
When all at once I saw a crowd,
A host, of golden daffodils;
Beside the lake, beneath the trees,
Fluttering and dancing in the breeze.

Continuous as the stars that shine
And twinkle on the milky way,
They stretched in never-ending line
Along the margin of a bay:
Ten thousand saw I at a glance,
Tossing their heads in sprightly dance.

The waves beside them danced; but they
Out-did the sparkling waves in glee:
A poet could not but be gay,
In such a jocund company:
I gazed—and gazed—but little thought
What wealth the show to me had brought:

For oft, when on my couch I lie
In vacant or in pensive mood,
They flash upon that inward eye
Which is the bliss of solitude;
And then my heart with pleasure fills,
And dances with the daffodils.

71. **What type of passage is the above selection?**

A. Lyrical poem

B. Haiku poem

C. Acrostic poem

D. Cinquain poem

72. **The permanence of stars as compared with flowers emphasizes**

A. the impermanence of life.

B. the permanence of memory for the poet.

C. the earlier comparison of the sky to the lake.

D. that stars are frozen above and daffodils dance below.

73. **The scheme of the poem is**

A. ballad.

B. Scottish stanza.

C. Spenserian stanza.

D. quatrain-couplet.

74. **This poem uses the _____ metric pattern.**

A. dactylic tetrameter

B. trochaic pentameter

C. trochaic tetrameter

D. iambic tetrameter

75. **What is a literary device used in the last two lines of the first two stanzas?**

A. Simile.

B. Metaphor.

C. Personification.

D. Allegory.

76. **In what literary period did this author write?**

   A. Edwardian Movement.

   B. Romanticism.

   C. Existentialism.

   D. Victorian Movement.

77. **As used in this poem, the best choice for a synonym of jocund means**

   A. pleasant.

   B. vapid.

   C. lonely.

   D. jovial.

78. **What literary device is used in line 9. "They stretched in never-ending line."**

   A. hyperbole.

   B. onomatopoeia.

   C. epithet.

   D. irony.

Questions 79-86. Read the following selection and answer the questions below, selecting the best choice of the options presented.

My Bondage and My Freedom

Disappearing from the kind reader, in a flying cloud or balloon (pardon the figure), driven by the wind, and knowing not where I should land—whether in slavery or in freedom—it is proper that I should remove, at once, all anxiety, by frankly making known where I alighted. The flight Disappearing from the kind reader, in a flying cloud or balloon (pardon the figure), driven by the wind, and knowing not where I should land--whether in slavery or in freedom--it is proper that I should remove, at once, all anxiety, by frankly making known where I alighted. The flight was a bold and perilous one; but here I am, in the great city of New York, safe and sound, without loss of blood or bone. In less than a week after leaving Baltimore, I was walking amid the hurrying throng, and gazing upon the dazzling wonders of Broadway. The dreams of my childhood and the purposes of my manhood were now fulfilled. A free state around me, and a free earth under my feet! What a moment was this to me! A whole year was pressed into a single day. A new world burst upon my agitated vision. I have often been asked, by kind friends to whom I have told my story, how I felt when first I found myself beyond the limits of slavery; and I must say here, as I have often said to them, there is scarcely anything about which I could not give a more satisfactory answer. It was a moment of joyous excitement, which no words can describe. In a letter to a friend, written soon after reaching New York. I said I felt as one might be supposed to feel, on escaping from a den of hungry lions.

79. **In what literary period did this author write?**

    A. Transcendentalism.

    B. Realism.

    C. Victorian.

    D. Naturalism.

80. **When the author writes "escaping from a den of hungry lions," what type of literary device is he using?**

    A. Simile

    B. Personification.

    C. Metaphor.

    D. Hyperbole.

81. **What is the author's theme in this passage?**

    A. Anger at being a slave.

    B. Numb, as one might be supposed to feel.

    C. Confusion at the new things he is seeing.

    D. Self-discovery after flight from slavery.

82. **In context of the passage, the opening phrase "to the kind reader" used by the author sets what kind of opening tone?**

    A. Friendly

    B. Condescending

    C. Boisterous

    D. Meek

83. **The author of this book relays his own experiences fighting slavery. Why does he fight against it (i.e. what is the theme of the book)?**

    A. Slavery is unnatural.

    B. Slavery wasn't needed as an economic engine.

    C. Slavery was morally acceptable.

    D. Slavery made time move too quickly.

84. **What does the author figuratively mean by "hurrying throng"?**

    A. The people that bump into him walking past him.

    B. His blurred vision from bright sunlight.

    C. The New York tradesmen rushing to their jobs.

    D. The bustling crowd of free people.

85. **What is the author's tone?**

    A. Cautious

    B. Enlightened

    C. Exuberant

    D. Nervous

86. **Who wrote this novel?**

    A. E.B. White

    B. Francis Scott

    C. Frederick Douglass

    D. Ralph Waldo Emerson

Questions 87-94. Read the following poem by Emily Dickenson and answer the questions below, selecting the best choice of the options presented.

IN THE GARDEN

A bird came down the walk:
He did not know I saw;
He bit an angle-worm in halves
And ate the fellow, raw.

And then, he drank a dew
From a convenient grass,
And then hopped sidewise to the wall
To let a beetle pass.

He glanced with rapid eyes
That hurried all abroad,—
They looked like frightened beads, I thought;
He stirred his velvet head

Like one in danger; cautious,
I offered him a crumb,
And he unrolled his feathers
And rowed him softer home

Than oars divide the ocean,
Too silver for a seam,
Or butterflies, off banks of noon,
Leap, splashless, as they swim.

87. What type of literary device is used in the author's phrase, "drank a dew"?

   A. Allusion.

   B. Foreshadowing.

   C. Juxtaposition.

   D. Alliteration.

88. The author describes action beginning in line 15 of the bird's flight. What type of literary device is used?

   A. Simile.

   B. Metaphor.

   C. Satire.

   D. None of these are correct.

89. The rhyme scheme of the poem (except the final three stanzas) is

   A. XAXA or Ghazal.

   B. Scottish stanza.

   C. Spenserian stanza.

   D. Petrarchan sonnet.

90. This poem uses a particular metric pattern throughout the poem, except in the third line of each stanza. What is the main metric pattern?

   A. dactylic tetrameter

   B. trochaic trimeter

   C. trochaic tetrameter

   D. iambic trimeter

91. What literary device is used when the bird's eyes are compared to frightened beads?

   A. Reverse Personification.

   B. Metaphor.

   C. Simile.

   D. Allegory.

92. **What does the dash at the end of line 12 represent?**

    A. A change in focus from the bird to the water.

    B. An abrupt change for the bird.

    C. An emotional shift from fear to fascination.

    D. It only shows the middle of the poem.

93. **What is the author's tone in this poem?**

    A. She takes the perspective of the bird.

    B. The author's tone is harsh toward potential prey.

    C. The tone is factual, describing the actions of a bird.

    D. The author's tone is gentle and respectful demeanor regarding nature.

94. **What is a potential meaning of the allegory used by the author?**

    A. It could reveal the author's perceptions of God.

    B. The author could reveal the hierarchy between man and beast.

    C. Descriptions of the forces of nature could parallel emotions.

    D. There is no allegory used as a literary device in this poem.

Questions 95-100. Read the following selection and answer the questions below, selecting the best choice of the options presented.

> There is no frigate like a book
> To take us lands away,
> Nor any coursers like a page
> Of prancing poetry;
> This traverse may the poorest take
> Without oppress of toll;
> How frugal is the chariot
> That bears the human soul!

95. **Authors use particular literary structures for descriptions. What best explains the type that Emily Dickinson employs in this poem?**

    A. Connotative

    B. Argumentative

    C. Narrative

    D. Rhetoric

96. **How many types of transport does the author incorporate?**

    A. Two

    B. Three

    C. Four

    D. None

97. **If the words 'frigate, coursers, and traverse' were replaced with synonyms, what would the best choice of the following options include?**

    A. Train, car, carriage

    B. Train, horse, carriage

    C. Ship, car, carriage

    D. Ship, horse, carriage

98. Which of the following descriptions more closely describes the author's intended meaning of poem?

   A. Difficulties at work

   B. The importance of books

   C. Confessions for the soul

   D. Poverty makes things difficult

99. There are very descriptive and strong feelings conveyed by the poet. Which of the following is not the definition of what she shares?

   A. Overstatement

   B. Sarcasm

   C. Understatement

   D. Irony

100. What kind of poetry form is utilized by Ms. Dickinson in this poem?

   A. Alexandrine

   B. Didactic poetry

   C. Ballad stanza

   D. Rondel

101. When students are given an assignment that is new to them, which of the following should almost always be discussed?

   A. What the students can expect to learn from doing the assignment.

   B. Whether the assignment will be graded in similar fashion to other assignments.

   C. Whether the students can expect to be tested on the material presented.

   D. The teacher's background with this type of assignment.

102. A high school classroom teacher is working with nonnative speakers of English. During class, students are asked to read aloud, and the teacher focuses on continuously correcting pronunciation errors. What has this teacher failed to take into account in regards to second language development?

   A. Reading skills must be established prior to learning the syntax of a language.

   B. The fastest way for a nonnative speaker is to imitate the way native speakers use the language.

   C. Students should never be asked to read out loud before they can read and comprehend grade appropriate texts silently.

   D. Nonnative speakers often understand what they are reading before they can accurately speak the language.

103. A middle school teacher gives her students a list of vocabulary words to use in their essay, intending for the list to act as a scaffold. If the students exhibit proficiency on a mastery level, which of the following would be the best 'next' step?

   A. Give the students advanced words, and more of them, to include in the next essay.

   B. Ask the students to work collectively to come up with a new list to use in the next essay.

   C. Ask students to use the same vocabulary words in the next essay as well.

   D. Give a new list of vocabulary terms and have them look up the definitions, then use them in the next essay.

104. An English teacher observes that a 10th grade student seems very upset about the idea of having to write a research paper. The teacher explains to the class as a whole, that the best approach for completing the assignment is to break the larger project into smaller tasks. Which of the following actions exemplify this methodology?

   A. Having students write about a familiar topic, then contrasting it with the topic for the research paper.

   B. Writing a rough draft of the paper, then handing it to a fellow student for feedback and a critical evaluation.

   C. Finding at least two credible sources for the research paper's topic, and seeing which aspects they both agree on.

   D. Compiling a bibliography of sources relating to the topic.

105. Why was it determined that students should be placed in the least restrictive educational environment?

   A. Because placement in a 'least restrictive environment' would normalize children with disabilities, as opposed to being educated in isolation from others.

   B. Because it was determined that classrooms should no longer be restrictive to minorities or females.

   C. Because it would reduce the fiscal cost of providing additional classrooms.

   D. Because adopting the least restrictive policies would increase funding to the school for special education.

106. In a crowded classroom with varying skill levels, how might the teacher best take advantage of the diversity of the learning styles?

   A. Separate the students by reading levels.

   B. Assess students individually, only, to mitigate potential anxiety for the students.

   C. Incorporate opportunities for multi-level interaction through reciprocal learning events.

   D. Assign students to learning centers for computer based learning.

107. **When introducing a classic work of fiction to 8th graders, what is a significant factor in its presentation and study?**

    A. Whether the student finds that he or she can relate to the material.

    B. Whether the material will include a test.

    C. The material must be drawn from modern fiction sources.

    D. Students must be able to read on grade level to be able to enjoy a classic work of literature.

108. **Classroom rules, when established correctly, require the teacher to do which of the following?**

    A. State the rules with a serious intent.

    B. Quickly establish authority in the classroom.

    C. Create as many rules as it takes to cover all of the possible issues that might arise.

    D. Explain why the rules are needed.

109. **If a teacher wanted to obtain data from a criterion-referenced test, as opposed to a norm-referenced test, which of the following would offer that information?**

    A. How much each student in the classroom already knows about a singular aspect of the subject.

    B. How much each student in the classroom knows about a singular aspect, as compared to other students on a national level.

    C. How much each student in the classroom knows as compared to other students in the district.

    D. How much each student in the classroom knows about a certain portion of the subject.

110. **Which of the following activities is a feature of an accelerated program as opposed to an enrichment activity?**

    A. Finishing an independent project.

    B. Participating in simulations, role playing, playing games.

    C. Taking an exam and receiving credit.

    D. Enrolling and completing a summer program.

111. **When characterizing a student's creativity, which of the descriptors are most apt?**

    A. The student's solution is applicable in many areas, not just one domain.

    B. The student's solutions, though seemingly unorthodox, upon further discovery prove sound.

    C. The student's solutions are a collection of false starts, some of which end up being relevant.

    D. The student's solutions do not deviate from the standard perspectives.

112. **When seeking to improve academic performance, as well as motivation of students, which of the following strategies are most likely to succeed?**

    A. Teachers appoint a liaison to work with the administration to create a 'best practices' set of rules.

    B. Teachers present material as a team, standardizing presentation, and mapping academic progress.

    C. Teacher collaboration to assess and monitor other classroom procedures offers successful solutions.

    D. The classroom teacher must utilize management techniques with which he is familiar and comfortable.

113. **For students learning the process of constructed response writing, what is the appropriate pedagogical process?**

    A. Independent writing (summative), guided writing (formative), model/shadowing

    B. Model/shadowing, guided writing (formative), independent writing (summative)

    C. Guided writing (formative), model/shadowing, independent writing (summative)

    D. Independent writing (summative), guided writing (formative), peer reviewed grouping

114. **An aspect of the reflective practice methodology is exemplified in which of the following?**

    A. The teacher limits the amount of peer review.

    B. The teacher should limit student input that challenges or questions established teaching practices.

    C. The teacher should allow peer review to take its natural course, offering very little framework to limit the problem solving process.

    D. The teacher should establish a safe environment that allows reflection to take place among an accepted practice that is applicable for all learning situations.

115. **When establishing the best way to assist students with comprehension skills, a teacher should focus on which of the following techniques as an informational text is read aloud?**

    A. Writing down questions as a text is read aloud

    B. Creating an outline

    C. Setting a purpose for reading

    D. Encouraging students to make predictions

116. **A teacher is planning a lesson on T.S. Eliot's "The Hollow Men" for his eleventh grade English class. This is an excerpt from the poem:**

    The eyes reappear
    As the perpetual star
    Multifoliate rose
    Of death's twilight kingdom
    The hope only
    Of empty men.

    What strategy, of those listed below, best allows for identification and understanding of the word 'multifoliate'?

    A. Structural analysis

    B. Contextual analysis

    C. Graphophonic analysis

    D. Syntactical analysis

117. **A teacher is working with a class that includes an ELL (English Language Learner) student. When assigning an informational essay to the class, which of the following techniques would assist the ELL in an understanding of the text?**

    A. Have all students create an illustration of some part of the text that they found interesting.

    B. Have the class use a graphic organizer to write down main ideas in the article.

    C. Hand out a list of most often used sentence stems to the entire classroom to use.

    D. Provide a list of words to the ELL that are familiar synonyms to the words that he or she is likely to encounter in the article assigned.

118. **An 8th grade English teacher notices that each day when she asks a couple of questions about the previous day's lesson, the same handful of students always answer. Which of the following would promote active engagement by a larger percentage of the students?**

    A. Encouraging those who are not answering, to do so.

    B. Allowing all students to create two questions about the day's assignment, to be asked the next day.

    C. Giving a participation grade that is not dependent on the correct answer.

    D. Having students evaluate their peers' responses using a rubric.

119. **Which of the following indicators would suggest that a student has developed strong communication skills when placed in a small group to discuss a novel?**

    A. Taking charge of the group and directing the conversation.

    B. Making comments that build upon statements made by others in the group.

    C. Asking questions of the group members that diverges from the topic of conversation.

    D. Asking whomever is talking to explain what they mean by their statements.

120. **In a high school classroom, a teacher has had students complete rough drafts of an expository essay, and has placed them in pairs to peer review each other's work. As a guideline, what should the teacher have students read to discern first?**

    A. Transitions

    B. Supporting details

    C. Biased language

    D. Varied sentence lengths

121. **A ninth grade English teacher is attempting to develop strategies that will promote a reading community in his classroom. Which of the following would be the least effective way of accomplishing this task?**

    A. Students bring in books from home to include in a classroom library.

    B. The teacher assigns book reports on books that are to be selected from a list.

    C. Students work with the teacher to create a list of favorite books to read.

    D. The teacher will institute a 'drop everything and read' program for thirty minutes each week.

122. **What best describes a type of formative evaluation for writing education?**

    A. Making careful readings of the text for mechanics, usage, spelling, and content.

    B. Marking mechanical errors with a colored pen.

    C. Asks students to turn in all work pertaining to the writing assignment, including outlines.

    D. Teacher makes comments on the goals that are being met by the student as the student works.

123. **When utilizing a computer in the classroom for writing assignments, the teacher must be aware of which of the following drawbacks when writing on a computer?**

   A. The writer may be unable to focus on the details and become distracted by the technology.

   B. The ability of a computer to quickly correct mistakes, often automatically, takes away from the aspect of writing that calls for reflection.

   C. Spell check programs do not assist students in learning to spell correctly, or select proper grammatical choices in their writing.

   D. Students tend to overlook glaring errors on the page because of the print type.

124. **When attempting to introduce a unit on poetry to freshmen students in a regular classroom, which of the following is the most ineffective technique?**

   A. Students are encouraged to bring their favorite song lyrics to class to discuss poetic devices used.

   B. Students will bring in their favorite poems to read aloud to the class.

   C. Students will work in groups to try to apply poetic devices in creating a popular song.

   D. Students will work in groups to illustrate a given poem.

125. **A new teacher is experiencing his first ELL student and wonders what type of activity would help this student the most. Which of the following might be suggested?**

   A. Provide the ELL student with more opportunities to write in English.

   B. Provide opportunities for the class, as well as the ELL student, to listen to the language via various media.

   C. Provide a wide range of activities that promote exposure to the language in all of its various modes (speaking, writing, reading).

   D. Make an assignment requiring students to make oral presentations in front of the class.

Questions 126-130. Read the following passage carefully before you decide on your answers to the questions.

Death, be not proud

Death, be not proud, though some have called thee
Mighty and dreadful, for thou art not so;
For those whom thou think'st thou dost overthrow
Die not, poor Death, nor yet canst thou kill me.
From rest and sleep, which but thy pictures be,
Much pleasure; then from thee much more must flow,
And soonest our best men with thee do go,
Rest of their bones, and soul's delivery.

Thou art slave to fate, chance, kings, and desperate men,
And dost with poison, war, and sickness dwell,
And poppy or charms can make us sleep as well
And better than thy stroke; why swell'st thou then?
One short sleep past, we wake eternally
And death shall be no more;
Death, thou shalt die.

126. **Who wrote this poem, titled "Death, be not Proud?"**

    A. John Donne

    B. William Shakespeare

    C. Emily Dickinson

    D. Edgar Allen Poe

127. **What type of poem is this?**

    A. Ballad

    B. Epic

    C. Prose

    D. Sonnet

128. **What is the rhyme scheme in the first stanza?**

    A. ABBAABBA

    B. AABBABBA

    C. ABCABCBC

    D. AABBCCAA

129. **What is the author implying in the following line?**

    "Die not, poor Death, nor yet canst thou kill me."

    A. He/She is invincible.

    B. His/Her soul will go to heaven; therefore, death does not end life.

    C. Death does not decide when he/she will die.

    D. Poor people do not decide when they will die.

130. **What does the following line represent?**

    "One short sleep past, we wake eternally"

    A. Being buried

    B. A coma

    C. Fighting off disease

    D. Resurrection

Section III: Answer Key

ANSWER KEY								
1. D	16. D	31. A	46. B	61. C	76. B	91. C	106. C	121. C
2. B	17. A	32. D	47. B	62. A	77. D	92. B	107. A	122. D
3. A	18. B	33. C	48. C	63. C	78. A	93. D	108. D	123. B
4. D	19. C	34. A	49. D	64. D	79. A	94. A	109. D	124. D
5. C	20. D	35. D	50. B	65. A	80. C	95. A	110. C	125. D
6. D	21. A	36. C	51. B	66. A	81. C	96. B	111. B	126. A
7. A	22. B	37. D	52. D	67. C	82. B	97. D	112. C	127. D
8. C	23. C	38. B	53. C	68. C	83. A	98. B	113. B	128. A
9. A	24. A	39. D	54. A	69. A	84. D	99. B	114. D	129. B
10. D	25. A	40. B	55. D	70. D	85. C	100. C	115. A	130. D
11. A	26. B	41. D	56. B	71. A	86. C	101. A	116. A	
12. B	27. D	42. D	57. D	72. B	87. D	102. D	117. D	
13. D	28. B	43. C	58. B	73. D	88. B	103. B	118. B	
14. D	29. B	44. C	59. C	74. D	89. A	104. C	119. B	
15. A	30. A	45. A	60. B	75. C	90. D	105. A	120. A	

Section IV: Answer Key with Rationales

1. In classic literature, which of the following do NOT represent the function of a character?

    A. Embody an idea

    B. Embody an ideal acting in the world

    C. Examine social conditions

    D. Present the setting

    The correct answer is D.

    While characters can contribute to the overall setting of a story, they are not THE setting for the story. The general purpose of a character is to support the plot and to move the story along. Therefore, the characters that have the most impact on the plot are those characters that are affected the most by events that happen in the story. Characters can do A-C, and most do, within the framework of a typical novel.

2. **Mrs. Samuels is wondering how she might best draw her seventh grade class into reading more deeply into the text as they begin their next novel study. Which of the following writing exercises would best contribute to critical reading skills?**

    A. Summarizing each paragraph as it is read.

    B. Doing a reflection on the chapter, connecting it to their own lives.

    C. Discussing the chapter in small groups.

    D. Drawing a scene from the book into a journal.

    The correct answer is B.

    Critical reading asks the student to look deeper into the text and making what they are reading meaningful. Research indicates that when students find something meaningful in what they are reading, the comprehension and interest levels rise significantly. While all of the other activities can contribute to a novel study, they do not ask the student do read critically in a way that will promote critical reading skills. A is incorrect because stopping after each paragraph to write down the main idea slows comprehension and the flow of the story. C and D both ask the student to do other activities aside from reading.

3. **Which of the following does not involve critical thinking?**

   A. Fill in the blank tests

   B. Summarizing

   C. Reflective essays

   D. Prediction of outcomes

   The correct answer is A.

   Asking a student to recall definitions or details does not involve critical thinking, and is on the lower level in Bloom's Taxonomy. The rest of the answers (B-D) involve higher levels of discernment, comprehension, and decision making.

4. **Mr. Trundle would like to do a close reading of the novel, The Outsiders, but isn't sure how to begin. Mrs. Smith meets with him to discuss the benefits of using New Criticism for the close reading. Which of the following will promote New Criticism close reading?**

   A. Taking notes while the teacher reads the text out loud.

   B. Learning about the author's overall intentions

   C. The setting and time in which the author wrote the work

   D. The literary text itself.

   The correct answer is D.

   New Criticism holds that the literary text, itself, is of greatest concern. All other extrinsic factors are inconsequential. Therefore, Mr. Trundle can promote a close reading by doing any number of projects which focus on the story, the text, itself.

5. **Which of the following literary theories, is based on moral and ethical teachings?**

   A. Structuralism

   B. New Criticism

   C. Moral Criticism

   D. Psychoanalytic Criticism

   The correct answer is C.

   Moral Criticism, as this form of criticism is based on the moral message of the literature. This form holds that the more moral the piece is, the better it is.

6. Which literary theory focuses on the inner workings and motivations of a character's actions?

   A. Moralism

   B. Deconstruction

   C. Marxism

   D. Psychoanalytical Criticism

The correct answer is D.

Psychoanalytical Criticism, and was based in large part on the work of Sigmund Freud. This theory analyzes the motivations of a character's actions and thought processes, and often allows the reader to predict what a character might do in the future.

7. **Mrs. Godwin has been reading about UDL (universal design for learning) and wants to create a lesson plan that would incorporate what she has learned. Which of the following characteristics would be inherent in a good UDL lesson plan?**

   A. Multiple avenues for students to interact with the material

   B. Worksheets that ask students to read the passage several times

   C. Listening to the teacher read the material, then taking a test

   D. Removing all technology and distractions from the classroom

The correct answer is A.

UDL lesson plans require the teacher to present the material visually, aurally, as well as texturally so that each student's learning style is addressed. B-D are incorrect because they limit the ways in which the student has to interact with the material. D is especially wrong because UDL uses technology in the classroom to make sure that all of the multiple venues are covered.

8. **According to Reif (1993) when students are presented with material, which of the following will result in the greatest retention of material?**

   A. Reading the material

   B. Seeing a skill performed

   C. Saying and doing a skill

   D. Hearing and seeing a skill

The correct answer is C.

This results in a 90% retention rate. Hearing and seeking a skill (D) is a close second with a 50% retention rate, while the other techniques have a much lower chance of engagement and retention.

Questions 9-16. Read the following selection and answer the questions below, selecting the best choice of the options presented.

> Two roads diverged in a yellow wood,
> And sorry I could not travel both
> And be one traveler, long I stood
> And looked down one as far as I could
> To where it bent in the undergrowth;
>
> Then took the other, as just as fair,
> And having perhaps the better claim,
> Because it was grassy and wanted wear;
> Though as for that the passing there
> Had worn them really about the same,
>
> And both that morning equally lay
> In leaves no step had trodden black.
> Oh, I kept the first for another day!
> Yet knowing how way leads on to way,
> I doubted if I should ever come back.
>
> I shall be telling this with a sigh
> Somewhere ages and ages hence:
> Two roads diverged in a wood, and I—
> I took the one less traveled by,
> And that has made all the difference.

9. **Who wrote this poem?**

    A. Robert Frost

    B. Emily Dickinson

    C. John Keats

    D. Emily Bronte

    The answer is A.

    Robert Frost is the author of this poem.

10. **When the author uses the phrase "wanted wear" in the third stanza, what does that mean?**

    A. It looked just as fair as the other path.

    B. It was not as inviting.

    C. The path didn't go the same way as the other one.

    D. The path was less traveled than the other one.

    The answer is D.

    One path had obviously been walked on, or "worn" more than the other. By stating that one of the paths "wanted wear," the author is implying that this path had not been trav-eled on often. Therefore, D is the best answer.

11. **The author says that he "took the one less traveled by"; what does that mean?**

    A. The other path looked like it was used more.

    B. He did the right thing when others chose the wrong one.

    C. He took the one on the left.

    D. He took the one on the right.

    The answer is A.

    Just as we learned in the previous question, one of the paths had been walked on far more frequently. The author took the one "less traveled by," meaning it had a minimal path already carved out. This makes A the best answer.

12. **What is another way the author states his path was the "one less traveled by"?**

    A. "both that morning equally lay"

    B. "no step had trodden black"

    C. "Somewhere ages and ages hence"

    D. "having perhaps the better claim"

    The answer is B.

    B is the only reference to travel, as the author suggests with a step.

13. **What does the author imply since he took the path less traveled?**

    A. He has run into fewer people that try to bully him into doing what they want.

    B. Life is tougher getting to see the light.

    C. He was sorry he didn't chose to go the more well-trod path.

    D. His life is better for choosing to go his own path.

    The answer is D.

    The author implies that he has had a better life due to the decisions that he's made on his own. He believes his life is better for choosing to go his own path.

14. **What is the rhyme scheme?**

    A. ABBAB

    B. ABABA

    C. ABAAC

    D. ABAAB

    The answer is D.

    This poem follows the ABAAB rhyme scheme.

15. **Taking the road less traveled by made all the difference because _____.**

    A. the decision shaped his life

    B. it was a good hike

    C. the character was able to find peace

    D. he created a new path on the road

    The answer is A.

    Going on the other path would have led to a different life for this character. The best answer is A because choosing the road less traveled by has been a decision that has shaped his life. While B, C, and D may have partial truths, A is the best answer for this question.

16. **What literary device is used in this poem?**

    A. Personification

    B. Propaganda

    C. Paradox

    D. Parallelism

    The answer is D.

    Because we know the path represents roads the author has taken in life, it's easy to determine that parallelism is the literary device used in this poem.

17. **Mr. Date notices that Emil, a new student from India, who has for the last few months been very quiet, has suddenly begun speaking with others in the classroom. While Mr. Date is glad that the others have accepted him, he notices that Emil is adjusting his speech patterns from correct English to non-standard English. He is worried that Emil will not learn to speak English correctly. In the preceding scenario, what is the behavioral action that Emil is engaged in, called?**

    A. Code-switching

    B. Peer integration

    C. Ebonics

    D. Colloquialism

    The correct answer is A.

    Emil has learned that the way his peers address one another is different from the way one addresses a teacher or someone outside of his peer group. New English language learners often have difficulty switching from one type of English to another, and apply informal language inappropriately. Mr. Date may need to address this in the near future if Emil does not figure this out, himself.

18. **Ms. Heisel prefers to show her class of English learners how to solve a problem, going step by step through the process, offering explanations along the way. Her method of teaching is which of the following?**

    A. Adjusting language of Instruction

    B. Explicit Teaching

    C. Providing Practice

    D. Goal oriented practice

    The correct answer is B.

    Explicit teaching as her technique is overtly teacher-led. The other techniques can be utilized in an English language classroom, but goals have to be clearly defined beforehand, and there must already be a foundation of acquired knowledge.

19. **Which of the following illustrates the benefits of the five paragraph essay formula?**

    A. Allow students to expand on topics with detail

    B. Utilizes outside sources

    C. Offers a way to develop instincts about structure

    D. Teaches the importance of a thesis statement

    The correct answer is C.

    The five paragraph essay not only gives students a framework from which to work, but allows them to experiment and develop their own unique voice, thesis statement, as well as a logical progression of information. Five paragraph essays, as a general rule, do not utilize outside sources such as a book report would, or a research paper. They are different types of writing. While A is technically correct, the five paragraph essay does more than create a way for students to add more detail to a topic, as a summary would. Thesis statements are important, but the five paragraph essay teaches more than just the importance of a well-crafted thesis.

20. **When grading students' essays, which of the following can cause flaws in reasoning which calls into question the efficacy of the entire essay?**

    A. Weak thesis statements

    B. Poor handwriting

    C. Misspelled words

    D. Unsupported conclusions

    The correct answer is D.

    This shows a lack of critical thinking when writing the paper. Students who do not understand the concept will often be technically perfect, but their reasoning is flawed, terms that they use may be vague, and they wander from the topic.

21. **Mr. Kirk wants to start using the computer lab more with his lower quartile students, but isn't sure what the best approach will be. Which of the following would work best to accomplish this goal?**

    A. Prepare a structured lesson plan with clear goals.

    B. Give students a long list and plenty of time to finish it.

    C. Make sure they all use headsets, to minimize distraction.

    D. Establish discipline and the rules before starting the project.

    The correct answer is A.

    A well-structured lesson plan anticipates and is proactive in providing the framework for the student to explore, but not become distracted. Specific, and limited goals are crucial to working with technology with students, especially the first few times. Giving long term project goals, initially, is a recipe for disaster, as is assuming that using headphones is going to cut down on the distraction. The teacher should have established classroom rules well before going into the classroom, so D is not the correct answer, either.

22. **What is one of the primary benefits of group writing?**

    A. Those that understand the process can assist those who are lagging.

    B. Students that are directly engaged with each other during the writing process will begin to challenge each other.

    C. Students will internalize structure.

    D. Students who work with others often learn new vocabulary words, and will incorporate them into their essays.

The correct answer is B.

Students will automatically compare their own writing to that of their peers, and will be motivated to learn how they accomplished it. Peer review is a very good way to motivate students to improve their writing. While very often those who are more accomplished will assist others, this is not the primary goal for group writing, but rather for others to gain additional ideas for how they might approach their own writing. Structures will be internalized whether they are in a group or not, and the focus is not on the structure in most group writing activities. Vocabulary may be learned in addition, but like structure, it is not the overall focus of a group writing exercise.

23. **One of the problems young writers have with the writing process is that the elaboration on a topic sentence is often lacking. Understanding this, Ms. Kenyon wants to use a research based approach to directly build up this skill. Which of the following would be the best choice for developing elaboration and supportive details in an essay?**

    A. Group writing

    B. Modeling

    C. Summarizing text

    D. Close reading

The correct answer is C.

It serves to teach them the value of clear and succinct writing, and how to assess which details are most essential to retain when describing something.

24. **Which of the following activities does NOT fall under the category of collaborative writing practices?**

    A. Computer based essay writing

    B. Brainstorming ideas

    C. Sharing their writing out loud

    D. Working in pairs

    The correct answer is A.

    Computer based writing is not a group activity, nor does it promote collaboration. Though students will eventually have to create an essay on computer, one of the best ways to get to the point where a student can work confidently alone is by first working with a partner, or a group.

Questions 25-32. Read the following selection and answer the questions below, selecting the best choice of the options presented.

"I went to work the next day, turning, so to speak, my back on that station. In that way only it seemed to me I could keep my hold on the redeeming facts of life. Still, one must look about sometimes; and then I saw this station, these men strolling aimlessly about in the sunshine of the yard. I asked myself sometimes what it all meant. They wandered here and there with their absurd long staves in their hands, like a lot of faithless pilgrims bewitched inside a rotten fence. The word 'ivory' rang in the air, was whispered, was sighed. You would think they were praying to it. A taint of imbecile rapacity blew through it all, like a whiff from some corpse. By Jove! I've never seen anything so unreal in my life. And outside, the silent wilderness surrounding this cleared speck on the earth struck me as something great and invincible, like evil or truth, waiting patiently for the passing away of this fantastic invasion.

—Heart of Darkness

25. **Who wrote this novel?**

    A. Joseph Conrad

    B. James Joyce

    C. Jane Austen

    D. Charles Dickens

    The answer is A.

    Joseph Conrad is the author of Heart of Darkness.

26. **What does the following line represent?**

    "I saw this station, these men strolling aimlessly about in the sunshine of the yard."

    A. Soldiers enjoying their day

    B. Men being unaware of the negativ,ity that surrounds them

    C. Positivity is infectious

    D. The station is a happy place

    The answer is B.

    The sunshine represents happiness and the fact that they are strolling around aimless-ly implies they are unaware of their surroundings. Given the representation of this symbolism, B is the best option for this question.

27. **What does the word staves mean?**

    A. Machete

    B. Axe

    C. Gun

    D. Wooden club

    The answer is D.

    Because of the invasion mentioned, it can be determined that the characters are walk-ing around with staves in order to protect themselves. Although each of the options for this question are weapons, D is the correct answer. It's a word that is most common to the time period in which this book was written.

28. **What does the ivory represent?**

    A. Death

    B. Prosperity

    C. Jewelry

    D. Trade

    The answer is B.

    Ivory has historically been very valuable. While it can be viewed as representing trade, D is incorrect because this piece includes symbolism. B is the best answer because ivory best repre-sents prosperity. A and C are easy to knock out as incorrect options.

29. **What literary device is used when describing the ivory?**

    A. Alliteration

    B. Allegory

    C. Simile

    D. Personification

    The answer is B.

    An allegory represents a piece of writing with hidden meaning or significant hidden symbolism. This is the only option that makes sense for this question.

30. **What does rapacity represent?**

    A. Greed

    B. Rapid movement

    C. Intelligent

    D. Generous

    The answer is A.

    Rapacity represents greed; therefore, A is the correct answer.

31. **What literary device is used in this passage?**

    "And outside, the silent wilderness surrounding this cleared speck on the earth struck me as something great and invincible, like evil or truth, waiting patiently for the passing away of this fantastic invasion."

    A. Simile

    B. Metaphor

    C. Illusion

    D. Onomatopoeia

    The answer is A.

    A simile is a comparison or description that uses "like" or "as." Because this passage uses "like evil or truth" to describe the wilderness, A is the best answer.

32. **Which style of writing is represented in this novel?**

    A. Biographical

    B. Autobiographical

    C. Expository

    D. Persuasive

The answer is D.

The story being told is fiction, so A and B can be eliminated from the start. C is incor-rect because the writing does not intend to give information. The writing is intended to persuade the reader, leaving D as the best answer.

33. **Which of the following is NOT one of the main factors that should be judged in every student's work?**

    A. Content

    B. Fluency

    C. Handwriting

    D. Syntax

The correct answer is C.

The content and structure of the essay is of greater importance. This is not to say that being unable to read someone's handwriting is not of importance, but when the focus is on the essay, then it must take a backseat to the content, structure, logical progression of ideas, and conventions.

34. **Ms. Gonzalez notices that Alisha, a new student who is from Pakistan, is having a difficult time fitting in. Which of the following is a good way to promote integration without focusing the attention directly on Alisha?**

    A. Discussing family holidays and traditions.

    B. Studying Pakistan and asking Alisha about it

    C. Reading a story from Pakistan

    D. Having Alisha teach some phrases in her native language to the students

The correct answer is A.

This is an all-inclusive way for all of the students to share something about themselves and their family without any one person being singled out. Bullying along ethnic lines can be detrimental to education and the mental health of the student and must be dealt with firmly. Students should find fascination in their backgrounds, not things to mock. All of the other answers focus the attention solely on Alisha, which misses the point of the activity all together.

35. Mr. Lawrence is grading some of his class's summaries and is feeling overwhelmed. While his students have completed the assignment, they have written longer than necessary paragraphs. How might he instruct his students on paring down their summaries?

    A. Have one of the students who has done it correctly, to be the teacher for the day.

    B. Show the students a sample summary that is correct.

    C. Ask them to write the main idea, only.

    D. Model the revision process, showing students how to determine the necessity of some details.

The correct answer is D.

When summaries are too long, it's because the student hasn't questioned the necessity of keeping a sentence or not. Asking themselves whether the sentence could go and not affect the summary as a whole, is a key critical thinking component, and will figure in later to the overall revision process for the essay.

36. Which of the following is a key transitional word to look for in informational texts written by students?

    A. Well

    B. So

    C. Furthermore

    D. Then

The correct answer is C.

Words that seem to indicate a maturity in writing is the adoption and use of upper level transition words or phrases, such as furthermore, as has been shown, or not only, but if, statements. First, second, next, then, and so, are all lower level transition words, and are good initially for developing structure, but later must be amended to a better selection of transition words and phrases.

37. **Mr. Reeder's eighth grade class has been invited to join Mrs. Kirby's ninth grade class to go see a performance of Romeo and Juliet at the local community college. To prepare for the field trip, they should:**

    A. Read an abbreviated version of the play and study listening skills

    B. Read a few important sections from the play to become familiar with Shakespearean language and style

    C. Assign the play to be read as a homework assignment

    D. Read a synopsis of the play in class and discuss

    The correct answer is D.

    This will give the students a quick idea of what the play is about, as well as generate excitement about attending the play. Shakespeare is not something that can be read overnight for a homework assignment, so C is not a viable choice. B, and A do not allow enough scope, in the amount of time given, to accomplish the goal.

38. **The Montgomery County High School English Department has decided to implement learning strategies that would encourage students to create student led reading communities. Which would be the best way to begin this process?**

    A. One set day a week each class would bring a book or magazine in and read for that class period.

    B. The class brainstorms as a group, suggesting books that they would like to share with the class, or study as a novel unit.

    C. Book reports are studied, and assigned.

    D. Each student contributes a book to the in-class library.

    The correct answer is B.

    The least effective would be C, because it does not foster or motivate students to read deeply. A and D are both viable options for after a program has been established.

39. **Which of the following is NOT a rhetorical writing strategy?**

    A. Satire

    B. Hyperbole

    C. Irony

    D. Theme

    The correct answer is D.

    While theme can be employed in an essay, it is not a rhetorical device. Rhetoric is used to make informative writing more interesting, and to persuade the reader to view something from the author's perspective.

40. **Mr. Cline has a lower quartile literature class of seniors. Which of the following teaching strategies would work best for motivating them to engage with the work more?**

    A. Allow group work, interactive panel discussions, portfolio creation, and many opportunities for hands-on applications.

    B. Allow students to select from a list which readings they would like to study.

    C. Practice 'popcorn' reading using an anthology

    D. Assign a list of vocabulary words

The correct answer is B.

This creates 'ownership' of the outcome and the students are invested in the course's design which they helped to create. C places stress on students who are already struggling and may not be proficient readers. Vocabulary words (D) is only rote memorization and does not accomplish the goal, while (A) is too much for lower quartile students to initially be involved with, especially if they are typically underachievers.

Questions 41-47. Read the following selection and answer the questions below, selecting the best choice of the options presented.

"Finished, it's finished, nearly finished, it must be nearly finished. Grain upon grain, one by one, and one day, suddenly, there's a heap, a little heap, the impossible heap. I can't be punished any more. I'll go now to my kitchen, ten feet by ten feet by ten feet, and wait for him to whistle me. Nice dimensions, nice proportions, I'll lean on the table, and look at the wall, and wait for him to whistle me."

—Endgame

41. **Who wrote this play?**

    A. Anton Chekov

    B. William Shakespeare

    C. Lillian Hellman

    D. Samuel Beckett

The answer is D.

Samuel Beckett is the author of Endgame.

42. **What literary device is used throughout this passage?**

    A. Simile

    B. Metaphor

    C. Euphemism

    D. Repetition

    The answer is D.

    Starting with the first line, repetition is an obvious literary device in this passage. Because nearly every statement includes repetition, D is the best answer for this question.

43. **What does the impossible heap represent**

    A. Life's greatest hurdles

    B. A pile of grain so tall it cannot be moved

    C. Death

    D. A mountain

    The answer is C.

    The impossible heap represents death. B is a literal interpretation of the setting, along with D. The symbolism throughout the selection lets the reader know that the end is near. There is no reference to life's hurdles or heaven, leaving C as the best answer.

44. **The whistle symbolizes _____.**

    A. A referee

    B. The character's father

    C. Death

    D. An angel

    The answer is C.

    Again, this selection is setting up a scene of the end of someone's life. A can quickly be eliminated, as there is no reference to sports. B would create a more positive, less drastic waiting period. Therefore, C is the correct answer.

45. **What is an endgame?**

    A. The final play in a game, such as chess

    B. The end of a negotiation

    C. A wish

    D. None of the above

    The answer is A.

    Because we know this passage represents the end of someone's life, the title is an obvious connection. An endgame represents the final play in a game, which is the best connection for this question.

46. **What is the author trying to portray in this selection?**

    A. An old man

    B. A prisoner

    C. A farmer

    D. A mill worker

    The answer is B.

    The passage does not incorporate any positive or happy references, therefore A can be eliminated. The character is not angry, and there are no implications that he/she is hungry, so C and D can be eliminated as well. The character is anxious and question-ing their punishment, which makes B the correct answer.

47. **What best describes this selection?**

    A. Epic

    B. Foreshadowing

    C. Cliffhanger

    D. Flashback

    The answer is B.

    The selection gives an idea of what's coming in the character's life, so B is the best answer. It is not climactic (C), and it does not look back throughout their life (D). The passage is not considered to be an epic (A).

48. **In an informative essay, which of the following should NOT be included in the introductory paragraph?**

    A. An attention getting device

    B. A general introduction to the topic

    C. Details that support the main idea of the essay

    D. A thesis statement

    The correct answer is C.

    In an introductory paragraph extraneous details tend to dilute the thesis statement. This makes for weak writing overall.

Questions 49-55. Read the following passage carefully before you decide on your answers to the questions.

O wild West Wind, thou breath of Autumn's being,
Thou, from whose unseen presence the leaves dead
Are driven, like ghosts from an enchanter fleeing,

Yellow, and black, and pale, and hectic red,
Pestilence-stricken multitudes: O thou,
Who chariotest to their dark wintry bed

The winged seeds, where they lie cold and low,
Each like a corpse within its grave, until
Thine azure sister of the Spring shall blow

Her clarion o'er the dreaming earth, and fill
(Driving sweet buds like flocks to feed in air
With living hues and odors plain and hill:

Wild Spirit, which art moving everywhere;
Destroyer and preserver; hear, oh, hear!

Thou on whose stream, 'mid the steep sky's commotion,
Loose clouds like earth's decaying leaves are shed,
Shook from the tangled boughs of Heaven and Ocean,

Angels of rain and lightning: there are spread
On the blue surface of thine aery surge,
Like the bright hair uplifted from the head

Of some fierce Maenad, even from the dim verge
Of the horizon to the zenith's height,
The locks of the approaching storm. Thou dirge

Of the dying year, to which this closing night
Will be the dome of a vast sepulchre,
Vaulted with all thy congregated might

Of vapors, from whose solid atmosphere
Black rain, and fire, and hail will burst: oh, hear!

49. **The first line of this poem exhibits what poetic devices?**
    I.   **Alliteration**
    II. **Personification**
    III. **Onomatopoeia**

    A. Only I

    B. Only II

    C. Only III

    D. I and II

    The answer is D.

    "Wild West wind" is an alliteration and "breath" is a personification of the wind the poem goes on to describe.

50. **What best describes the final stanza of this selection?**

    A. Slant rhyme

    B. Heroic couplet

    C. Hyperbole

    D. Irony

    The answer is B.

    The final line is a classic heroic couplet, it contains an AA rhyme and has ten syllables per line. "Rhyme" is too vague for this question (A), and it exhibits no hyperbole (C), or irony (D).

51. **"Wild Spirit, which art moving everywhere; Destroyer and preserver; hear, oh, hear!"**

    This passage displays a…

    A. Enjambment

    B. Slant rhyme

    C. Simile

    D. Iamb

    The answer is B.

    "Everywhere" and "hear" are not "true" rhymes, though they are close. The selection features no enjambment (A), simile (C), or iamb (D).

52. **This poem is written in what style?**

    A. Vers libre

    B. Heroic couplet

    C. Epic saga

    D. Iambic pentameter

    The answer is D.

    The piece features ten syllables per line divided into five iambs, suggesting similarities to a sonnet.

53. **What in the poem is compared to "Angels of rain and lightning"?**

    A. The wind

    B. Maenads

    C. Clouds

    D. Human souls

    The answer is C.

    Two lines earlier the poem describes "loose clouds" which are later likened to angels of rain and lightning.

54. "Of the dying year, to which this closing night/ Will be the dome of a vast sepulchre,/ Vaulted with all thy congregated might"

This passage exhibits…

A. A metaphor

B. An allegory

C. A comparison

D. An allusion

The answer is A.

A metaphor is the best way to describe this passage, as it suggests the "closing night" will be the "dome of a vast sepulcher", without a comparative term such as "like" or "as".

55. **How many stanzas does this poem contain?**

A. Four

B. Five

C. Eight

D. Ten

The answer is D.

There are ten stanzas, though they are irregular in terms of line count.

56. **Which is the most important issue to be aware of when utilizing computer based writing of essays?**

A. The writer can tend to focus only on completing the task, rather than spending time on the supportive details.

B. The technology makes it very easy to make corrections quickly, and removes the facet of contemplation from the writing process.

C. The proofreading function does not allow students to catch their own mistakes and fix them.

D. The print looks so clean and clear that students do not see their mistakes.

The correct answer is B.

Contemplative writing, pausing to review what has been written, being able to see what has been stricken through, is part of the process of shaping an essay. Computers remove the text completely, make corrections automatically, and often don't allow for a writer to stop and ponder the next thought.

Use the following introduction from a student essay for the following questions.

(1) When reading this poem it is clear that there are two stories going on. (2) First, it is a story of a man finding an ancient statue half buried in the sands. (3) The traveler who finds the statue comes away with a new way to view life, in general, and so does the reader. (4) This poem is the author's way of showing that time does not respect anything manmade, that it is all temporary and can go away to be forgotten.

57. **In the sample essay, which of the sentences provides the thesis?**

    A. Sentence 1

    B. Sentence 2

    C. Sentence 3

    D. Sentence 4

The correct answer is D.

While the reader may be tempted to select Sentence 3 as the thesis, it is really Sentence 4 that blatantly sums up the point that the writer is trying to make, and will be building upon in the rest of the essay.

58. **Which of the sentences in the provided sample provide detail?**

    A. Sentence 1

    B. Sentence 2

    C. Sentence 3

    D. Sentence 4

The correct answer is B.

The detail supports the main idea of the paragraph, which is that a traveler has found a statue, and because of this discovery has an epiphany about man's place in the world.

59. **Which of the following is NOT a common logical fallacy?**

    A. Appeal to Authority

    B. Slippery Slope

    C. Exposition

    D. Straw man

The correct answer is C.

Exposition is the expanding of a topic sentence with elaboration, which can include rhetoric, logical fallacies, and any number of other details.

60. **Many junior high school students have trouble distinguishing between correlation and causation. A lack of understanding about these two distinct properties can lead to poor persuasive writing, because the essence of an argument is not understood. Which of the following would lay the groundwork for better persuasive essay writing?**

    A. Purposely writing false correlations as a class

    B. Analyzing short scenarios for false correlations and causations

    C. Discussing the definitions of correlation and causation

    D. Read about false correlations on the internet

    The correct answer is B.

    Students often do not understand how a correlation can be determined to be false. Showing many examples, modeling the thought process first, then allowing students as a group, and then as individuals, to find the false correlations, is the best way to make them aware of it, and transfer that awareness to their writing. A does not work because they do not yet understand what a false correlation is. C and D provide knowledge, but no practical application.

61. **Of the following statements, which is most true in regards to expository essays?**

    A. Summative evaluations work best when scoring.

    B. Should always be formal

    C. Should incorporate other forms of discourse when providing elaboration

    D. This type of essay writing is exclusive to other forms of discourse.

    The correct answer is C.

    Involving other forms of discourse will allow the reader to become involved with the text, as well as the writer.

62. **When evaluating the media, what does the appearance of sighs, laughs, eye rolls, tears, or even overt expressions of shock or outrage from the reporter, indicate about news that is being delivered?**

    A. That the news is colored by the personal opinions of the reporters.

    B. That the news is trustworthy.

    C. That the news is opinion based and not fact based

    D. That the news station is trying to push their own agenda

    The correct answer is A.

    Sighs, laughs, eye rolls, tears, or even overt expressions of shock personalize the news reports, often to the point of slanting the news in one direction. However, this does not make the news untrustworthy, but rather indicates that the viewer must exercise some critical listening and viewing skills to ascertain the truth of a matter.

63. **Media bias is an important topic to a contemporary audience. In order to discuss and teach a unit on this subject, what of the following is a good activity?**

    A. Giving a lecture on the topic.

    B. Having a reporter come to speak to the class

    C. Watch a newscast that features two political candidates and analyze how it is presented.

    D. Hand out a worksheet about media bias, then have students watch the nightly newscast to analyze it.

    The correct answer is C.

    Though D seems like a likely selection as well, the students do not yet have enough framework and reference to do the analysis on their own. Likewise, students can see how one candidate may have a news story about some scandal or unlikely donation, while the focus on the other candidate revolves around a positive attribute or action, indicating bias.

64. **Which of the following statements is incorrect in regards to media in the classroom?**

    A. The internet makes it possible for students to reach beyond their own regional culture and location to connect with others on a global scale.

    B. Educational media can make certain topics more powerful when utilized correctly.

    C. Virtual reality experiences provide students a chance to experience information unavailable to them in their current circumstance.

    D. Teachers should be judicious in their use of media in the classroom, due to the saturation of students by media at home.

    The correct answer is D.

    In fact, teachers must reach students where their interest levels lie, and for most students, that is with current technology.

65. **Of the following statements, which statement about multimedia in the classroom offers a specific goal?**

    A. Teachers can engage their students by offering opportunities to foster a critical perspective toward audiovisual presentations.

    B. Students who listen to an audio book have less interaction than those who simply read the passages themselves.

    C. Reading text engages students to think more deeply about what it is they are reading.

    D. Mental images are formed when an audio message/book is listened to.

    The correct answer is A.

    Students who are given specific goals when interacting with multimedia engage more readily.

66. **Which of the following statements is not a fallacy in logic?**

    A. All students in Ms. Sanders' class have failed a grade. Misha is in Ms. Sanders' first period. Misha has failed a grade.

    B. All students who have failed a grade are in Ms. Sanders' class. Misha is in Ms. Sanders' first period class. Misha has failed a grade.

    C. Misha has failed a grade. Misha is in Ms. Sanders' first period class. All students in Ms. Sanders' first period class have failed a grade.

    D. If Misha has failed a grade, then she is a grade ahead. Misha is in Ms. Sanders' class. Misha has not failed a grade.

    The correct answer is A.

    The rest of the statements involve statements that cannot be proven, or are incomplete associations, causations, or connections.

67. **Mr. Hill's 10th grade class wants to create a webcast about the devastation of Hurricane Matthew, and utilize some multimedia in their creation of the webcast. Which of the following would be the best choices for making the presentation more effective?**

    A. A PowerPoint slideshow with before and after photos.

    B. Music clips from the devastated areas, both before and after the hurricane.

    C. Video footage of the devastation as well as the rebuilding efforts

    D. Interviews of different officials in the area, as well as those affected by the storm.

    The correct answer is C.

    Video footage and striking imagery can do more than the other suggestions, combined. The other suggestions have before and after clips, which are also effective, but if the goal is to depict the devastation of the area, then C is the better choice.

68. **Of the following issues, which would not be as much of an issue with an oral presentation?**

    A. Making sure the purpose for the presentation is clear.

    B. Needing to know the audience's particular tastes and proclivities

    C. Creating a Powerpoint slide to correspond with each point

    D. Creating the content to fit the specific occasion.

    The correct answer is C.

    Most oral presentations use PowerPoint to correspond with the points, and while knowing an audience's preferences, or needing to tailor the presentation are important, the least issue is C.

69. **Of the following writing techniques, which would allow students to improve the cohesion of the ideas in a persuasive essay?**

    A. Key transitional words that show relationship between one idea to another

    B. Using conjunctions to link ideas

    C. Using quotes to offer validity

    D. Increasing the amount of adjectives and adverbs to make the detail more vivid

    The correct answer is A.

    Being armed with a collection of easily accessible transitional words gives young writers the tools to logically connect ideas and to flow from one argument to the next.

70. **Use the following statements to answer the following question:**

    The teachers at NM High are confident in their ability to teach English at a high level. Staff at NMHS always welcome new ideas for presenting the material.

    In order to show contrast between these two ideas in a persuasive essay, which of the following transition words would be the best insertion?

    A. The teachers at NMHS are confident in their ability to teach English, and always welcome new ideas for presenting material.

    B. Because the teachers at NMHS are confident, they welcome new ideas.

    C. When the teachers at NMHS are confident about their abilities, they welcome new ideas.

    D. NMHS English teachers and staff are confident in their ability to teach at a high level; however, they also welcome new ideas for presenting material.

    The correct answer is D.

    If the goal is to show contrast between the two ideas of confidence, and accepting new ideas. The others link them together, so as to show commonality.

Questions 71-78. Read the following passage carefully before you decide on your answers to the questions.

William Wordsworth — "I Wandered Lonely As A Cloud"

I wandered lonely as a cloud
That floats on high o'er vales and hills,
When all at once I saw a crowd,
A host, of golden daffodils;
Beside the lake, beneath the trees,
Fluttering and dancing in the breeze.

Continuous as the stars that shine
And twinkle on the milky way,
They stretched in never-ending line
Along the margin of a bay:
Ten thousand saw I at a glance,
Tossing their heads in sprightly dance.

The waves beside them danced; but they
Out-did the sparkling waves in glee:
A poet could not but be gay,
In such a jocund company:
I gazed—and gazed—but little thought
What wealth the show to me had brought:

For oft, when on my couch I lie
In vacant or in pensive mood,
They flash upon that inward eye
Which is the bliss of solitude;
And then my heart with pleasure fills,
And dances with the daffodils.

71. **What type of passage is the above selection?**

   A. Lyrical poem

   B. Haiku poem

   C. Acrostic poem

   D. Cinquain poem

The correct answer is A.

This is where literary terms are important. In poetry, many of the devices and nomenclature need to be memorized and understood so you can answer these questions quickly and accurate.

72. **The permanence of stars as compared with flowers emphasizes**

   A. the impermanence of life.

   B. the permanence of memory for the poet.

   C. the earlier comparison of the sky to the lake.

   D. that stars are frozen above and daffodils dance below.

The correct answer is B.

The key word in option A is opposite in meaning and the relationship of the verbs in D are not correctly aligned for the comparison. If you don't know the answer between B and C, look back at the poem - and there is no comparison of sky to lake, so that gives you the right answer.

73. **The scheme of the poem is**

    A. ballad.

    B. Scottish stanza.

    C. Spenserian stanza.

    D. quatrain-couplet.

    The correct answer is D.

    While this may not be one of the typical questions on the test, it is incorporated so you remember to look at general literary definitions. You can also figure this out by looking at quatrain, which has the base that means "four" and couplet means "two" - that is the same pattern as the poem. E isn't right because a sonnet is one verse of specific length; a ballad is the manner of telling a story so it isn't A. There are particular components of B and C, but if you get to this stage and use the root words, you may be able to guess the right answer if you don't know.

74. **This poem uses the _____ metric pattern.**

    A. dactylic tetrameter

    B. trochaic pentameter

    C. trochaic tetrameter

    D. iambic tetrameter

    The correct answer is D.

    Similar to the rationale of the first question, you need to know these terms. You can "break them down" into tetra - meaning four - and meter, or beat. Iambic is a rhythm of two, so there are four sets of two beats

75. **What is a literary device used in the last two lines of the first two stanzas?**

    A. Simile.

    B. Metaphor.

    C. Personification.

    D. Allegory.

    The correct answer is C.

    When an inanimate or non-human objects is given person-like traits, it's call personification. You should be familiar with all of the words that are given as options in this multiple choice question - review them in the guide for refresher.

76. **In what literary period did this author write?**

   A. Edwardian Movement.

   B. Romanticism.

   C. Existentialism.

   D. Victorian Movement.

   The correct answer is B.

   In an AP situation, your understanding of when great writers of literature wrote, and the context of their writing - when they wrote - often gives additional insights to the meaning of their work or the themes.

77. **As used in this poem, the best choice for a synonym of jocund means**

   A. pleasant.

   B. vapid.

   C. lonely.

   D. jovial.

   The correct answer is D.

   This is a question that tests vocabulary - you should be able to eliminate choices A and C. If you don't know what jocund means, or either vapid or jovial, this is how they are testing for reading comprehension. Jovial is happy and that fits into the structure of the passage within context.

78. **What literary device is used in line 9. "They stretched in never-ending line."**

   A. hyperbole.

   B. onomatopoeia.

   C. epithet.

   D. irony.

   The correct answer is A.

   Knowing what common literary terms mean will allow you to eliminate D, if not also B. Between C and A, you could guess, but if you understand either of the definitions, you will pick the correct answer. Review definitions if you can't eliminate at least three of the word answer choices.

Questions 79-86. Read the following selection and answer the questions below, selecting the best choice of the options presented.

My Bondage and My Freedom

Disappearing from the kind reader, in a flying cloud or balloon (pardon the figure), driven by the wind, and knowing not where I should land—whether in slavery or in freedom—it is proper that I should remove, at once, all anxiety, by frankly making known where I alighted. The flight Disappearing from the kind reader, in a flying cloud or balloon (pardon the figure), driven by the wind, and knowing not where I should land--whether in slavery or in freedom--it is proper that I should remove, at once, all anxiety, by frankly making known where I alighted. The flight was a bold and perilous one; but here I am, in the great city of New York, safe and sound, without loss of blood or bone. In less than a week after leaving Baltimore, I was walking amid the hurrying throng, and gazing upon the dazzling wonders of Broadway. The dreams of my childhood and the purposes of my manhood were now fulfilled. A free state around me, and a free earth under my feet! What a moment was this to me! A whole year was pressed into a single day. A new world burst upon my agitated vision. I have often been asked, by kind friends to whom I have told my story, how I felt when first I found myself beyond the limits of slavery; and I must say here, as I have often said to them, there is scarcely anything about which I could not give a more satisfactory answer. It was a moment of joyous excitement, which no words can describe. In a letter to a friend, written soon after reaching New York. I said I felt as one might be supposed to feel, on escaping from a den of hungry lions.

79. **In what literary period did this author write?**

   A. Transcendentalism.

   B. Realism.

   C. Victorian.

   D. Naturalism.

   The correct answer is A.

80. **When the author writes "escaping from a den of hungry lions," what type of literary device is he using?**

   A. Simile

   B. Personification.

   C. Metaphor.

   D. Hyperbole.

   The correct answer is C.

81. **What is the author's theme in this passage?**

    A. Anger at being a slave.

    B. Numb, as one might be supposed to feel.

    C. Confusion at the new things he is seeing.

    D. Self-discovery after flight from slavery.

    The correct answer is C.

    The author is in a storm of new sensations.

82. **In context of the passage, the opening phrase "to the kind reader" used by the author sets what kind of opening tone?**

    A. Friendly

    B. Condescending

    C. Boisterous

    D. Meek

    The correct answer is B.

    If you were answering too quickly, you may think A is the correct answer. But look at the context. The speaker is pandering to the listener.

83. **The author of this book relays his own experiences fighting slavery. Why does he fight against it (i.e. what is the theme of the book)?**

    A. Slavery is unnatural.

    B. Slavery wasn't needed as an economic engine.

    C. Slavery was morally acceptable.

    D. Slavery made time move too quickly.

    The correct answer is A.

    There is no proof that the author believes B is true, nor any of the other answers. Remember, it's not what you believe but what the author is stating or leading you to believe and that's how you must answer. If you read too fast, you may have thought B was the correct answer, but notice the answer is actually negative. Read carefully.

84. **What does the author figuratively mean by "hurrying throng"?**

    A. The people that bump into him walking past him.

    B. His blurred vision from bright sunlight.

    C. The New York tradesmen rushing to their jobs.

    D. The bustling crowd of free people.

    The correct answer is D.

    The middle two options are not correct, but A could possibly be accurate. However, there is nothing in the passage that should lead you to think he was bumped into by people passing him. Don't make assumptions or you won't select the right answer.

85. **What is the author's tone?**

    A. Cautious

    B. Enlightened

    C. Exuberant

    D. Nervous

    The correct answer is C.

    While the feeling of the character may be D, there are more cues that point to C being the right answer.

86. **Who wrote this novel?**

    A. E.B. White

    B. Francis Scott

    C. Frederick Douglass

    D. Ralph Waldo Emerson

    The correct answer is C.

    Some of the main pieces of literature are listed for you in the book, and it would be wise to know some of the main and often used authors and their high profile works.

Questions 87-94. Read the following poem by Emily Dickenson and answer the questions below, selecting the best choice of the options presented.

IN THE GARDEN

A bird came down the walk:
He did not know I saw;
He bit an angle-worm in halves
And ate the fellow, raw.

And then, he drank a dew
From a convenient grass,
And then hopped sidewise to the wall
To let a beetle pass.

He glanced with rapid eyes
That hurried all abroad,—
They looked like frightened beads, I thought;
He stirred his velvet head

Like one in danger; cautious,
I offered him a crumb,
And he unrolled his feathers
And rowed him softer home

Than oars divide the ocean,
Too silver for a seam,
Or butterflies, off banks of noon,
Leap, splashless, as they swim.

87. **What type of literary device is used in the author's phrase, "drank a dew"?**

A. Allusion.

B. Foreshadowing.

C. Juxtaposition.

D. Alliteration.

The correct answer is D.

These are all basic literary device words and you should know the definitions of these most-frequently used terms.

88. **The author describes action beginning in line 15 of the bird's flight. What type of literary device is used?**

    A. Simile.

    B. Metaphor.

    C. Satire.

    D. None of these are correct.

    The correct answer is B.

    Remember, absolute answers, such as ones that give "always" or "never" or "none" are typically incorrect. Of the remaining options, you should know these definitions, especially the difference between simile and metaphor.

89. **The rhyme scheme of the poem (except the final three stanzas) is**

    A. XAXA or Ghazal.

    B. Scottish stanza.

    C. Spenserian stanza.

    D. Petrarchan sonnet.

    The correct answer is A.

    Even if you don't know the terms (which you should have memorized for poetry), the pattern is usually listed for you. As long as you know how to use those abbreviations, you can get any poetry scheme question correct.

90. **This poem uses a particular metric pattern throughout the poem, except in the third line of each stanza. What is the main metric pattern?**

    A. dactylic tetrameter

    B. trochaic trimeter

    C. trochaic tetrameter

    D. iambic trimeter

    The correct answer is D.

    Using the logic explained in earlier rational, iambic is "rhythm of two and tri- means three. You should be able to get to the root of any of these words and determine the correct answer if you don't know it, so practice!

91. **What literary device is used when the bird's eyes are compared to frightened beads?**

    A. Reverse Personification.

    B. Metaphor.

    C. Simile.

    D. Allegory.

    The correct answer is C.

    While these types of questions are not likely to come back-to-back in the actual exam, they were placed in repetitive order here to show you that you need to remain focus, answer each question and move forward.

92. **What does the dash at the end of line 12 represent?**

    A. A change in focus from the bird to the water.

    B. An abrupt change for the bird.

    C. An emotional shift from fear to fascination.

    D. It only shows the middle of the poem.

    The correct answer is B.

    In context, the bird goes from drinking and allowing a beetle to pass to abruptly being wary. That is the opposite of C, but many students who rush through the test may select that option. Literally, D is not accurate nor is A.

93. **What is the author's tone in this poem?**

    A. She takes the perspective of the bird.

    B. The author's tone is harsh toward potential prey.

    C. The tone is factual, describing the actions of a bird.

    D. The author's tone is gentle and respectful demeanor regarding nature.

    The correct answer is D.

    If you know basics about various authors, you would know that Ms. Dickenson wrote during an era of respecting nature and promoting its good features to the masses.

94. **What is a potential meaning of the allegory used by the author?**

    A. It could reveal the author's perceptions of God.

    B. The author could reveal the hierarchy between man and beast.

    C. Descriptions of the forces of nature could parallel emotions.

    D. There is no allegory used as a literary device in this poem.

    The correct answer is A.

    Knowing your definitions, D can be removed as correct because you would have identified the allegory previously. While C is a fair choice, A is a better one - again, known the traits of the era, you would be able to most easily identify the right choice.

Questions 95-100. Read the following selection and answer the questions below, selecting the best choice of the options presented.

There is no frigate like a book
To take us lands away,
Nor any coursers like a page
Of prancing poetry;
This traverse may the poorest take
Without oppress of toll;
How frugal is the chariot
That bears the human soul!

95. **Authors use particular literary structures for descriptions. What best explains the type that Emily Dickinson employs in this poem?**

    A. Connotative

    B. Argumentative

    C. Narrative

    D. Rhetoric

    The correct answer is A.

    You need to know the definitions of literary terms.

96. **How many types of transport does the author incorporate?**

    A. Two

    B. Three

    C. Four

    D. None

    The correct answer is B.

    You can see the next question to identify the three options.

97. **If the words 'frigate, coursers, and traverse' were replaced with synonyms, what would the best choice of the following options include?**

    A. Train, car, carriage

    B. Train, horse, carriage

    C. Ship, car, carriage

    D. Ship, horse, carriage

    The correct answer is D.

    You can see them listed in the poem.

98. **Which of the following descriptions more closely describes the author's intended meaning of poem?**

    A. Difficulties at work

    B. The importance of books

    C. Confessions for the soul

    D. Poverty makes things difficult

    The correct answer is B.

    The main idea of the poem is stated in the first line.

99. There are very descriptive and strong feelings conveyed by the poet. Which of the following is not the definition of what she shares?

   A. Overstatement

   B. Sarcasm

   C. Understatement

   D. Irony

The correct answer is B.

The other four selections are used at various times in the poem and you must read carefully as the question asks for the one that isn't used.

100. **What kind of poetry form is utilized by Ms. Dickinson in this poem?**

   A. Alexandrine

   B. Didactic poetry

   C. Ballad stanza

   D. Rondel

The correct answer is C.

You should be able to eliminate B and D immediately. Alexandrine is a French style that has twelve syllables. If you didn't know that, and you probably won't, a ballad stanza is four line verses - and that should be enough to get it right.

101. **When students are given an assignment that is new to them, which of the following should almost always be discussed?**

   A. What the students can expect to learn from doing the assignment.

   B. Whether the assignment will be graded in similar fashion to other assignments.

   C. Whether the students can expect to be tested on the material presented.

   D. The teacher's background with this type of assignment.

The correct answer is A.

According to many studies, students learn best when they are motivated. To be motivated, students must draw conclusions that are meaningful and worthwhile, leading toward larger goals instead of performance goals. By discussing why something is being done, and what they can gain from learning it, students will be more motivated to attempt something new.

102. **A high school classroom teacher is working with nonnative speakers of English. During class, students are asked to read aloud, and the teacher focuses on continuously correcting pronunciation errors. What has this teacher failed to take into account in regards to second language development?**

   A. Reading skills must be established prior to learning the syntax of a language.

   B. The fastest way for a nonnative speaker is to imitate the way native speakers use the language.

   C. Students should never be asked to read out loud before they can read and comprehend grade appropriate texts silently.

   D. Nonnative speakers often understand what they are reading before they can accurately speak the language.

The correct answer is D.

Learning should focus on comprehension and formal accuracy, as well as usage.

103. **A middle school teacher gives her students a list of vocabulary words to use in their essay, intending for the list to act as a scaffold. If the students exhibit proficiency on a mastery level, which of the following would be the best 'next' step?**

   A. Give the students advanced words, and more of them, to include in the next essay.

   B. Ask the students to work collectively to come up with a new list to use in the next essay.

   C. Ask students to use the same vocabulary words in the next essay as well.

   D. Give a new list of vocabulary terms and have them look up the definitions, then use them in the next essay.

The correct answer is B.

Scaffolding is, at best, a temporary framework to assist students toward the goal of being independent learners. Thus, once the skill has been mastered, the scaffold needs to be withdrawn. Having the students become responsible for providing their own vocabulary words not only withdraws the scaffold, but it encourages independent, as well as reciprocal, learning. None of the other answers meet these two criteria.

104. **An English teacher observes that a 10th grade student seems very upset about the idea of having to write a research paper. The teacher explains to the class as a whole, that the best approach for completing the assignment is to break the larger project into smaller tasks. Which of the following actions exemplify this methodology?**

A. Having students write about a familiar topic, then contrasting it with the topic for the research paper.

B. Writing a rough draft of the paper, then handing it to a fellow student for feedback and a critical evaluation.

C. Finding at least two credible sources for the research paper's topic, and seeing which aspects they both agree on.

D. Compiling a bibliography of sources relating to the topic.

The correct answer is C.

A larger task can often overwhelm a student, so breaking the task into smaller subtasks is a way of lessening a student's anxiety about a long term assignment. Both A and B involve creating the whole work first, and D is still a large task and may only serve to overwhelm the student further.

105. **Why was it determined that students should be placed in the least restrictive educational environment?**

A. Because placement in a 'least restrictive environment' would normalize children with disabilities, as opposed to being educated in isolation from others.

B. Because it was determined that classrooms should no longer be restrictive to minorities or females.

C. Because it would reduce the fiscal cost of providing additional classrooms.

D. Because adopting the least restrictive policies would increase funding to the school for special education.

The correct answer is A.

The idea of 'least restrictive' was based on the legislation that stated that the education of divergent learners, and learners with disabilities should only be segregated if necessary, and that permanent placement within a regular classroom setting would be of more benefit to all students. The legislation is based on P.L 94-142.

106. **In a crowded classroom with varying skill levels, how might the teacher best take advantage of the diversity of the learning styles?**

   A. Separate the students by reading levels.

   B. Assess students individually, only, to mitigate potential anxiety for the students.

   C. Incorporate opportunities for multilevel interaction through reciprocal learning events.

   D. Assign students to learning centers for computer based learning.

   The correct answer is C.

   Students who work within varying level environments all benefit. Those who are in the lower quartile may be motivated or encouraged by their peers, while those who are in the upper quartile will synthesize the material in a way that allows them to apply what they have learned.

107. **When introducing a classic work of fiction to 8th graders, what is a significant factor in its presentation and study?**

   A. Whether the student finds that he or she can relate to the material.

   B. Whether the material will include a test.

   C. The material must be drawn from modern fiction sources.

   D. Students must be able to read on grade level to be able to enjoy a classic work of literature.

   The correct answer is A.

   Many studies exist which indicate that students who are interested, and who feel that the material has some relevance to their lives will be motivated to learn a subject. Literature whose themes and relevancy to modern life are indicated by the teacher can play a significant factor in the successful completion of a unit of study.

108. **Classroom rules, when established correctly, require the teacher to do which of the following?**

   A. State the rules with a serious intent.

   B. Quickly establish authority in the classroom.

   C. Create as many rules as it takes to cover all of the possible issues that might arise.

   D. Explain why the rules are needed.

   The correct answer is D.

   Classroom management is achieved by having a few rules that make sense to students. When students in this age group are given reasons for the rules, they are more likely to comply.

109. **If a teacher wanted to obtain data from a criterion-referenced test, as opposed to a norm-referenced test, which of the following would offer that information?**

    A. How much each student in the classroom already knows about a singular aspect of the subject.

    B. How much each student in the classroom knows about a singular aspect, as compared to other students on a national level.

    C. How much each student in the classroom knows as compared to other students in the district.

    D. How much each student in the classroom knows about a certain portion of the subject.

    The correct answer is D.

    Criterion-referenced tests determine the comprehension of a specific competency. These types of tests judge the student against the standard, and not against others in the state, nation, or district. Since the goal is to determine comprehension and knowledge, a group based performance (norm referenced) is not indicated. A is not the answer because it does not measure the student's gained knowledge, only knowledge that was preexisting.

110. **Which of the following activities is a feature of an accelerated program as opposed to an enrichment activity?**

    A. Finishing an independent project.

    B. Participating in simulations, role playing, playing games.

    C. Taking an exam and receiving credit.

    D. Enrolling and completing a summer program.

    The correct answer is C.

    Students who take an exam and are able to receive credit for that class, or subject, are able to CLEP or skip out of that class. Thus, they have accelerated their learning process. The other options offer students enrichment activities designed to supplement learning.

111. **When characterizing a student's creativity, which of the descriptors are most apt?**

    A. The student's solution is applicable in many areas, not just one domain.

    B. The student's solutions, though seemingly unorthodox, upon further discovery prove sound.

    C. The student's solutions are a collection of false starts, some of which end up being relevant.

    D. The student's solutions do not deviate from the standard perspectives.

    The correct answer is B.

    With the exception of B, the other answers are common misconceptions about creative thinkers. Divergent thinkers typically arrive at their conclusions from different perspectives and angles.

112. **When seeking to improve academic performance, as well as motivation of students, which of the following strategies are most likely to succeed?**

    A. Teachers appoint a liaison to work with the administration to create a 'best practices' set of rules.

    B. Teachers present material as a team, standardizing presentation, and mapping academic progress.

    C. Teacher collaboration to assess and monitor other classroom procedures offers successful solutions.

    D. The classroom teacher must utilize management techniques with which he is familiar and comfortable.

The correct answer is C.

When teachers collaborate, share experiences, and assess one another on a routine basis, all are made stronger and benefit from the collaboration. New teachers often benefit from a veteran teacher's experience, while the veteran teacher can benefit by embracing new techniques and processes employed by the new teacher.

113. **For students learning the process of constructed response writing, what is the appropriate pedagogical process?**

    A. Independent writing (summative), guided writing (formative), model/shadowing

    B. Model/shadowing, guided writing (formative), independent writing (summative)

    C. Guided writing (formative), model/shadowing, independent writing (summative)

    D. Independent writing (summative), guided writing (formative), peer reviewed grouping

The correct answer is B.

Writing is a skill and as such must be presented in a logical manner, and in a manner which does not promote student anxiety or apprehension. Thus, showing the students how something is written, having them imitate the process, then guiding them through the process, culminating in independent attempts is the best method for acquisition of a new skill, in particular, writing.

114. **An aspect of the reflective practice methodology is exemplified in which of the following?**

    A. The teacher limits the amount of peer review.

    B. The teacher should limit student input that challenges or questions established teaching practices.

    C. The teacher should allow peer review to take its natural course, offering very little framework to limit the problem solving process.

    D. The teacher should establish a safe environment that allows reflection to take place among an accepted practice that is applicable for all learning situations.

    The correct answer is D.

    Trust is the foundation upon which peer review and reflective practice must be built. B and C are useful only in a limited capacity, as creativity may be hampered. The classroom teacher must establish a set context upon which each assignment will draw, especially when peer interaction, reflection, or critique are involved.

115. **When establishing the best way to assist students with comprehension skills, a teacher should focus on which of the following techniques as an informational text is read aloud?**

    A. Writing down questions as a text is read aloud

    B. Creating an outline

    C. Setting a purpose for reading

    D. Encouraging students to make predictions

    The correct answer is A.

    If a student is able to write down questions about what is being read, then comprehension must follow. This type of metacognition is evident when a relevant question is asked about the text that is read. C and D are used as pre-reading strategies.

116. A teacher is planning a lesson on T.S. Eliot's "The Hollow Men" for his eleventh grade English class. This is an excerpt from the poem:

> The eyes reappear
> As the perpetual star
> Multifoliate rose
> Of death's twilight kingdom
> The hope only
> Of empty men.

What strategy, of those listed below, best allows for identification and understanding of the word 'multifoliate'?

A. Structural analysis

B. Contextual analysis

C. Graphophonic analysis

D. Syntactical analysis

The correct answer is A.

Structural analysis is the most effective way to analyze the prefix, and the root. Graphophonic requires a student to create a definition based on the sounds, and does not provide enough context for figuring out the meaning of the word. B is partially useful only in that the word, rose, offers some clues to the meaning of the word, but it does not offer enough context to come to a determination of its meaning. Syntactical analysis (D) is incorrect because this type of analysis will only determine that the word in question is being used as an adjective and nothing more.

117. A teacher is working with a class that includes an ELL (English Language Learner) student. When assigning an informational essay to the class, which of the following techniques would assist the ELL in an understanding of the text?

A. Have all students create an illustration of some part of the text that they found interesting.

B. Have the class use a graphic organizer to write down main ideas in the article.

C. Hand out a list of most often used sentence stems to the entire classroom to use.

D. Provide a list of words to the ELL that are familiar synonyms to the words that he or she is likely to encounter in the article assigned.

The correct answer is D.

The answer is D because the ELL is provided some context for the words that he or she is likely to encounter in the reading. Sentence stems (C) may be helpful when the ELL begins to write but it does not assist with comprehension in reading. (B) is incorrect because the student would have to already have an understanding of the content and context. (A) is incorrect because it does not perpetuate language development comprehension.

118. **An 8th grade English teacher notices that each day when she asks a couple of questions about the previous day's lesson, the same handful of students always answer. Which of the following would promote active engagement by a larger percentage of the students?**

    A. Encouraging those who are not answering, to do so.

    B. Allowing all students to create two questions about the day's assignment, to be asked the next day.

    C. Giving a participation grade that is not dependent on the correct answer.

    D. Having students evaluate their peers' responses using a rubric.

    The correct answer is B.

    Having students create a bank of questions each day allows the teacher to use questions from students whom do not normally risk answering a question. Not only does this promote interaction, but it also creates an opportunity for students to create relevant questions, and adds one more evaluative model for a teacher to assess comprehension.

119. **Which of the following indicators would suggest that a student has developed strong communication skills when placed in a small group to discuss a novel?**

    A. Taking charge of the group and directing the conversation.

    B. Making comments that build upon statements made by others in the group.

    C. Asking questions of the group members that diverges from the topic of conversation.

    D. Asking whomever is talking to explain what they mean by their statements.

    The correct answer is B.

    While many of the other answers may be indicators of someone who is able to communicate, (B) indicates that the student not only comprehends what is being said, but is also able to be a constructive listener. (C) is incorrect because students who diverge from the topic at hand are not effectively listening. (A) is incorrect because the student may be more interested in garnering attention without furthering the goal of the group, while (D) is incorrect because if someone is asking for a lot of explanation it is clear that they are not listening, or that there may be comprehension issues.

120. **In a high school classroom, a teacher has had students complete rough drafts of an expository essay, and has placed them in pairs to peer review each other's work. As a guideline, what should the teacher have students read to discern first?**

A. Transitions

B. Supporting details

C. Biased language

D. Varied sentence lengths

The correct answer is A.

While all of these are good aspects to evaluate, the first to be evaluated should be the use of adequate transitions. If a student has used transitions, shifts from one idea to the next, then the student has internalized the concept of 'flow' and 'voice' within their writing. The other aspects must certainly be considered, but as a first evaluative assessment, (A) is the starting point.

121. **A ninth grade English teacher is attempting to develop strategies that will promote a reading community in his classroom. Which of the following would be the least effective way of accomplishing this task?**

A. Students bring in books from home to include in a classroom library.

B. The teacher assigns book reports on books that are to be selected from a list.

C. Students work with the teacher to create a list of favorite books to read.

D. The teacher will institute a 'drop everything and read' program for thirty minutes each week.

The correct answer is C.

(C) is the least likely technique to improve or promote a sense of community as it is teacher-centric rather than student-centric. Students are motivated and readily participate on a larger percentage when there has been active participation in the process. Additionally, (D) is a type of modelling behavior where the teacher actively promotes reading for enjoyment, and it opens up a ready platform for a dialogue about reading, thus motivating reluctant readers to attempt reading more frequently.

122. **What best describes a type of formative evaluation for writing education?**

    A. Making careful readings of the text for mechanics, usage, spelling, and content.

    B. Marking mechanical errors with a colored pen.

    C. Asks students to turn in all work pertaining to the writing assignment, including outlines.

    D. Teacher makes comments on the goals that are being met by the student as the student works.

The correct answer is D.

In formative evaluation the teacher continues to give insight to the student on those goals that are being met, thus supporting behaviors and skills that are wanted, and focusing on achieving the goal rather than focusing on those skills that are lacking.

123. **When utilizing a computer in the classroom for writing assignments, the teacher must be aware of which of the following drawbacks when writing on a computer?**

    A. The writer may be unable to focus on the details and become distracted by the technology.

    B. The ability of a computer to quickly correct mistakes, often automatically, takes away from the aspect of writing that calls for reflection.

    C. Spell check programs do not assist students in learning to spell correctly, or select proper grammatical choices in their writing.

    D. Students tend to overlook glaring errors on the page because of the print type.

The correct answer is B.

One of the largest components of learning to write is to take the time to consider what will be written. Because of various social media interactions, the quick aspect of the computer to automatically correct problems, the contemplation factor is removed, and the process of revising may break down.

124. **When attempting to introduce a unit on poetry to freshmen students in a regular classroom, which of the following is the most ineffective technique?**

    A. Students are encouraged to bring their favorite song lyrics to class to discuss poetic devices used.

    B. Students will bring in their favorite poems to read aloud to the class.

    C. Students will work in groups to try to apply poetic devices in creating a popular song.

    D. Students will work in groups to illustrate a given poem.

The correct answer is D.

Students may enjoy illustrating a poem, but it does not facilitate or accomplish the goal. The goal is to encourage students to learn to appreciate poetry and to try to write their own poems. Allowing students to bring in poems that they already like, or song lyrics they are familiar with, are better methods for promoting interest and motivating students to attempt the new skill.

125. **A new teacher is experiencing his first ELL student and wonders what type of activity would help this student the most. Which of the following might be suggested?**

    A. Provide the ELL student with more opportunities to write in English.

    B. Provide opportunities for the class, as well as the ELL student, to listen to the language via various media.

    C. Provide a wide range of activities that promote exposure to the language in all of its various modes (speaking, writing, reading).

    D. Make an assignment requiring students to make oral presentations in front of the class.

The correct answer is D.

While this may be initially a difficult assignment, the ELL student will benefit from hearing the language and thus understand phonologically the differences in the sounds. Correlations and contextual meanings of words are understood when heard and viewed, than when read.

Questions 126-130. Read the following passage carefully before you decide on your answers to the questions.

Death, be not proud

Death, be not proud, though some have called thee
Mighty and dreadful, for thou art not so;
For those whom thou think'st thou dost overthrow
Die not, poor Death, nor yet canst thou kill me.
From rest and sleep, which but thy pictures be,
Much pleasure; then from thee much more must flow,
And soonest our best men with thee do go,
Rest of their bones, and soul's delivery.

Thou art slave to fate, chance, kings, and desperate men,
And dost with poison, war, and sickness dwell,
And poppy or charms can make us sleep as well
And better than thy stroke; why swell'st thou then?
One short sleep past, we wake eternally
And death shall be no more;
Death, thou shalt die.

126. **Who wrote this poem, titled "Death, be not Proud?"**

   A. John Donne

   B. William Shakespeare

   C. Emily Dickinson

   D. Edgar Allen Poe

   The correct answer is A.

   John Donne is the author of this poem.

127. **What type of poem is this?**

   A. Ballad

   B. Epic

   C. Prose

   D. Sonnet

   The correct answer is D.

   This poem is a sonnet. All sonnets have iambic pentameter. The Haiku is made up of a short poem with specific syllables per line. Prose is told in story form and does not always rhyme. The ballad is free verse, often set to music.

128. **What is the rhyme scheme in the first stanza?**

    A. ABBAABBA

    B. AABBABBA

    C. ABCABCBC

    D. AABBCCAA

    The correct answer is A.

    By looking over the words that rhyme in the first stanza, it's easy to determine the rhyme scheme as ABBAABBA.

129. **What is the author implying in the following line?**

    "Die not, poor Death, nor yet canst thou kill me."

    A. He/She is invincible.

    B. His/Her soul will go to heaven; therefore, death does not end life.

    C. Death does not decide when he/she will die.

    D. Poor people do not decide when they will die.

    The correct answer is B.

    The author implies that although death may be the end of their body on earth, their soul will live on in heaven. Therefore, B is the best option.

130. **What does the following line represent?**

    "One short sleep past, we wake eternally"

    A. Being buried

    B. A coma

    C. Fighting off disease

    D. Resurrection

    The correct answer is D.

    This is a straightforward question: the words "wake" and "eternally" are direct connections to resurrection.

Interested in dual certification?

XAMonline offers over 30 Praxis study guides which are aligned to current standards and provide a comprehensive review of the core test content. Want certification success on your first exam? Trust XAMonline's study guides to help you succeed!

Praxis Series:

- **Middle School English Language Arts**
  9781607873457
- **English to Speakers of Other Languages**
  9781607876267
- **Principles of Learning and Teaching 7-12**
  9781607876250
- **Principles of Learning and Teaching K-6**
  9781607876243
- **School Guidance and Counseling**
  9781607870678
- **Social Studies: Content Knowledge**
  9781607874652
- **Special Education 0354/5354, 5383, 0543/5543 [Book and Online]**
  9781607874157
- **Special Education: Core Knowledge and Applications**
  9781607876281
- **Educational Leadership: Administration and Supervision**
  9781607873297
- **Elementary Education: Multiple Subjects**
  9781607874607

- **English Arts: Content Knowledge**
  9781607876274
- **Mathematics: Content Knowledge**
  9781607876298
- **Middle School Mathematics**
  9781607876304
- **Middle School Social Studies**
  9781607873440
- **Middle School Science**
  9781607873433
- **ParaPro Assessment**
  9781607870524
- **Physical Education**
  9781607870715
- **Chemistry**
  9781581976915
- **General Science**
  9781607873495
- **Social Studies**
  9781607873426
- **Biology**
  9781607873464
- **Spanish**
  9781607870869

Don't see your test? Visit our website: www.xamonline.com

XAMonline.com